HOT AND SPICY
COOKBOOK

Photography by Peter Barry
Watercolour illustrations by Sally Brewer
Designed by Julie Smith and Helen Johnson
Edited by Kate Cranshaw

CLB 4359
This edition published 1995 by Simon & Schuster
© 1995 CLB Publishing, Godalming, Surrey
All rights reserved
Colour separations by Tien Wah Press, Singapore
Printed and bound in Singapore
ISBN 0-671-71429-5

HOT AND SPICY
COOKBOOK

EDITED BY KATE CRANSHAW

SIMON & SCHUSTER

LONDON · SYDNEY · NEW YORK · TOKYO · SINGAPORE · TORONTO

Contents

Introduction

Spices have been used as flavourings ever since humans first began cooking and preserving their food. Because cave paintings rarely depict plants we do not know how early their various properties were discovered. In addition to adding strong, pungent flavours to foods and making even the most bland ingredient taste interesting, it was soon found that spices had medicinal uses and their preservative powers were vitally important before refrigeration. Spices are still used as medicines both in orthodox medicine and in herbal and alternative therapies. Spices are an essential ingredient in pickling and preserving, and those that produce bright colours are also used as dyes.

For five thousand years, the spice trade was dominated by the Arabs, since Arabia is conveniently situated on the trade routes midway between the source of the spices and their biggest customers, the Europeans. Even the Greeks and Romans believed that such rare and costly spices as ginger, pepper, nutmeg, mace, saffron, coriander and cumin, which in reality came from central and south-east Asia, were grown in the swamps of Africa. The Arab traders told all kinds of other tall tales of how difficult it was to collect and extract the spices, in order to protect their sources. In this way, they could pretend that they were not merely middlemen but actually the growers and exporters. So when Lady Macbeth mentions 'the perfumes of Arabia' she (and Shakespeare) did not realise that the perfumes, which were all made from spices, came not from the deserts of the Middle East but from India, Malaysia, Indonesia and the Moluccas (also known as the Spice Islands). Even after Rome fell, the Arab trade continued to flourish since Europe was more isolated than ever from the source of the spices that it needed so badly. The Prophet Mohammed himself traded in spices. Although the Arabs did not grow the rarest of the spices themselves, it was they who invented the techniques for distilling and storing them, and extracting their scents and essential oils.

Even as early as Roman times, Europeans suspected that the Arabs were being less than honest about the source of their wealth. In AD 40, a Greek merchant discovered the secret of the Trade Winds in the Indian Ocean which bore the Arab ships eastwards to the Spice Islands in the summer and westwards to Arabia again in the winter. From then on, the Europeans tried to capture this most lucrative trade for themselves, venturing into distant waters in search of the precious spice cargoes which were worth more than their weight in gold. In the Middle Ages, two pounds of mace cost the same as a cow, and people could pay their rent in peppercorns, hence the expression 'a peppercorn rent', which in those days represented a large sum of money.

The spice trade is responsible for some notable achievements in history. Marco Polo made his trip from Venice to China in the early 13th century to buy spices, and Venice dominated the spice trade thereafter. It was to find a quicker passage to India and thus easy access to spices that Columbus set sail in 1492. Although he did not find the spices of the Orient, he discovered a whole new range of flavours which have enriched the world's palate ever since and transformed its cooking techniques. It is difficult to imagine what Hungarian cooking was like without its precious paprika, and to realise that the chilli powders of India and the small red peppers of south-east Asia were not part of those cuisines until the 16th century. And what would our puddings taste like without vanilla and that great product of the cocoa bean, chocolate?

What is a Spice?

Spices were traditionally defined as rare and costly ingredients to be used sparingly. When first introduced, cane sugar was classified as a spice! Strictly speaking a spice is a strongly-flavoured substance derived from the roots and/or seeds of a plant, rather than its stems and leaves. Flavourings from the stems and leaves are usually defined as herbs. There is often a very close link or even an overlap between the definitions of a spice and a herb. The green parts of coriander, for instance, are used as a herb, while the seeds are used as a spice. Cinnamon and cassia are the inner bark of a tree, but they are definitely spices and not herbs. Curiously, the odd perception has lingered in alternative medicine that while herbs are 'medicinal' and healthy, spices are somehow unhealthy. Thus, in herbal guides, caraway and aniseed, for instance, are often described as herbs when plainly it is the seeds which are of

medicinal use, so technically they are spices. Similarly, liquorice is thought of as a herb, although it is extracted from the roots of the plant.

Spice Mixtures

It was soon discovered that spice blends often produced an even better result in cookery than the use of individual spices. In Europe, we tend to produce sweet spice mixtures for flavouring puddings, cakes and biscuits. Ginger, mace, nutmeg, cinnamon and cloves are combined and sold as 'mixed spice', in France there is the 'quatre épices' mixture used for Spice Cake (Pain d'épices) and in the Netherlands and Belgium, a special mixture is made for flavouring the crisp little spice biscuits known as Spekulaasjes or Speculeuses. In the United States a similar mixture is sold as 'pumpkin pie spice'. Sweet spices such as these are used to flavour meat dishes in Greece and the Near East; it is surprising what a difference a pinch of allspice, cinnamon or mixed spice will make to a beef or lamb stew.

In cold climates spices were also used to increase the warming effects of alcoholic and non-alcoholic drinks. Mulled wine and the traditional Christmas drink of egg nog spiced with nutmeg were very popular. A posset was a hot milk drink to which spices and sometimes alcohol were added, and which was drunk at bed-time. Special containers, known as posset pots, were used to keep the drink warm until it was to be drunk. Spiced wines, such as Glühwein, are still popular in ski resorts in Europe and the U.S.A.

In hot countries, spice mixtures tend to be of the savoury variety. A special mixture called *ras al-hanout*, consisting of more than 20 spices, dominated by the flavours of cayenne pepper and ground coriander, is used for flavouring couscous, a dish of wheat grains and meat eaten in North Africa. The Indians make various spice mixtures for flavouring curries of which the best known are curry powder, so-called because the curry leaf is an ingredient, and garam masala. Both of these are used to flavour the savoury meat dishes which have acquired the name of their spicy flavourings. Garam masala has the predominant flavour of ground cumin seed but contains many other spices.

Chilli powder is a spice mixture in which, obviously, chillies predominate. It is not the same as cayenne pepper which consists of pure ground powdered chillies. Indian chilli powder has a strong flavour of cumin whereas Mexican chilli powder contains a lot of ground coriander seed. Five-spice powder, the favourite Chinese spice mixture, contains a high proportion of star anise and Szechuan pepper, fennel, cloves and cinnamon in smaller quantities. Five-spice powder is popular not just in China but in much of south-east Asian cookery.

The most important use for spice mixtures throughout the ages has been for pickling. Pickling spices are used in combination with large quantities of salt to impart flavour to preserved meats and vegetables, and are added to sugar to preserve fruits. Peppercorns, allspice, chillies and fennel are important savoury pickling spices. Allspice, ginger, cinnamon and cloves are used in sweet pickles and preserves. Pickling spices are usually used whole.

Liquid Spices

Perhaps because of the ease of transporting and preserving the flavour of spices, spice-importing countries favour the use of spices distilled in liquid. All the popular table or 'brown' sauces – Worcestershire Sauce, OK Sauce, HP Sauce, and even tomato ketchup – are really spice mixtures in a liquid medium. In North America, such sauces tend to be hot and fiery, based on the hottest and smallest chilli peppers. The best-known and most imitated is Tabasco sauce, made on an island off the coast of Louisiana. The Brazilians and Portuguese use a sauce flavoured with tiny red hot peppers called Piri-piri and in Jamaica there is Pickapeppa Sauce. All of these should be used very sparingly as condiments.

Spices are also distilled into essential oils, but these are used mainly medicinally and therapeutically. The oil of cloves remedy for toothache is particularly well-known and so effective that dentists recommend it over and above proprietary pain-killers. Spice oils are not used much in home cooking as they are too highly concentrated, with the exception of vanilla which is distilled and mixed with alcohol to make an essence.

Buying and Storing Spices

Spices are such an important ingredient that they should always be kept on hand for emergencies. In addition to black pepper, a supply of nutmeg, cloves and cinnamon should feature in the store cupboard. Always buy spices in small packs, loose spices look very attractive on sale but the exposure to air causes them to lose their aroma and freshness. Keep the packs away from the light. If you have a spice rack, put it on a wall that is out the sunlight and do not use glass spice jars unless you keep them in a dark cupboard, china or enamel are best. When using black or white pepper in recipes try to use freshly-ground peppercorns straight from the pepper mill, they are much more aromatic than the ready-ground variety.

Indian cooks always advocate grinding your own spices freshly and for special occasion curries it is a good idea to do this. Some spices which do not need fine grinding, such as peppercorns, can be crushed in a pestle and mortar. If you prefer your spices more finely ground, there are electric spice mills on the market, or use a coffee grinder, preferably one kept for the purpose. You can also use spices to flavour coffee. Cardamom seeds, cinnamon stick or vanilla bean ground up with your usual coffee beans will impart a delicious aroma to your next brew.

Some spice seeds, such as fenugreek, coriander, cumin and poppy seed, benefit from being heated before being pounded, ground or used whole. While the convenience of buying ready-ground spices cannot be denied, where possible it is best to buy the whole spice and grate or grind it as needed. The aroma of freshly-ground pepper and freshly-grated nutmeg or root ginger cannot compare to the shop-bought, pre-ground product. Some spices are hard to grind finely at home, of course, such as cloves, and so must be bought ready-ground or, as in the case of ginger, the ground product is slightly different from the fresh and is used in a different way.

Preparing the Ingredients

Because spices are strong flavours, they are also irritants. When handling spices it is therefore advisable to wear disposable gloves. If you should get spice dust or chilli juice on a sensitive spot, wash it away with plenty of warm water. Some of the main methods of preparing ingredients, such as chillies, are shown opposite.

Chillies

Always wash your hands after preparing chillies and even then, do not touch your eyes or other sensitive areas for several hours thereafter. To add a mild flavour to dishes, chillies can be used whole, but the majority of recipes call for sliced chillies. The whole chilli can be finely sliced crossways into thin rings, or for those who prefer all of the flavour with less of the heat, the chillies can be deseeded. Use a small sharp knife to slice the chilli open lengthways [1], wearing disposable rubber gloves to protect your fingers from the chilli juice. Scrape out the seeds with the tip of the knife [2], then slice the chilli into thin shreds or finely chop.

Ginger

For the best flavour make sure the ginger you buy is fresh, choose firm pieces with smooth, unwrinkled skin. Peel off the skin of the ginger using a vegetable peeler or a paring knife [3]. The ginger can be used whole and fried in oil to add a mild flavour to a dish, sliced thinly and cut into fine shreds, or finely grated [4]. Only peel and prepare the amount of ginger required for the recipe, store any remaining fresh ginger in the refrigerator.

Lemon Grass

To use lemon grass, cut off the hard root and the grassy top. Remove and discard the tough outer leaves. To release the flavour, bruise the stem with a heavy knife by pressing down hard on the side of the blade [5], add whole to dishes and remove before serving. To impart more flavour, thinly slice the central tender core before adding.

Saffron Strands

When using saffron threads, rather than powder, the saffron needs preparing before being added to a dish to ensure that its full flavour and colour are imparted. The dried threads should be crushed in a pestle and mortar, then soaked in a little warm liquid, such as water, stock, or wine, depending on the recipe.

Tamarind

The juice of the tamarind pulp needs to be extracted before it can be used. Soak the pulp in double its volume of warm water for 20-30 minutes, mashing the pulp occasionally against the side of the bowl. Strain the mixture through a sieve, pressing all the juice out of the pulp with the aid of a spoon [6]. Scrape the underside of the sieve and add to the liquid.

Whole Spices

Whole spices often need to be ground before use. Use either a pestle and mortar [7] and crush then pound the ingredients, or use an electric spice mill or coffee grinder, grinding small quantities at once and processing in bursts. Do not use a coffee grinder that you use for coffee as the strong flavours will taint the beans. Once the spices have been ground they may need to be fried before adding to a dish, this is usually included in the recipe. Dry-frying spices allows their full flavour to develop, although care should be taken as the spices need only a minute or two and can easily burn. Watch the frying pan and stir the spices constantly to ensure even heat distribution [8]. If a recipe calls for spices to be fried in oil, be sure to fry them over a low heat as the oil will heat up very quickly and if the spices burn they will impart a bitter flavour to the final dish.

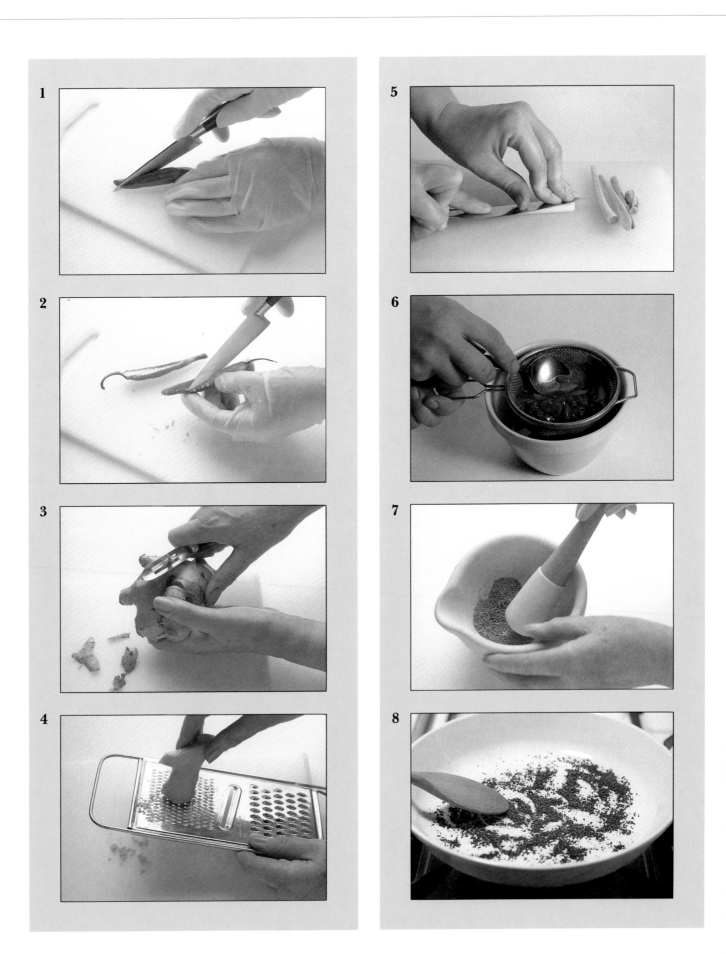

Glossary

The following are some of the spices used in this book, with some additional suggestions for using them:-

Allspice (Jamaica pepper) – these black berries taste like a mixture of nutmeg, cloves and cinnamon. They are native to central America and the West Indies and even today are grown nowhere else. Ground allspice can be used just like ground mixed spice in sweet and savoury dishes. The whole berries are an important ingredient in pickling spice and are used to flavour Benedictine and Chartreuse liqueurs.

Mustard seeds (black, brown or white) – mustard is one of the few spices which has long been grown in Britain though it originates from the Mediterranean. Black and white mustard need to be grown in different types of soil, but generally favour sandy soils. The seeds of the brown and white varieties are blended to make English mustard, but the ground seeds of the black variety are used exclusively in French mustard, and give it its darker colour. The seeds are only "hot" when blended with water. Whole black mustard seed is used in Indian cookery, largely for flavouring breads.

Caraway – caraway and cumin seeds are often confused with each other because they look alike, but the flavour is completely different. Caraway originates from the Middle East but it is most popular in central Europe where it is eaten at almost every meal in the form of a rye bread flavoured with caraway seeds. Caraway is used to flavour Hungarian goulash and German dumplings and even in a liqueur called Kümmel, the German name for caraway. Caraway seed cake was popular in England in Victorian times, though it now seems to have gone out of fashion, perhaps because the flavour is not popular in this form.

Cardamom – the tiny black cardamom seeds are sweetly aromatic. They come encased in a fibrous pod which may be green, bleached white or black. This book contains recipes using all three types of cardamom pod. The pods can be lightly crushed at one end, and then split open a little and added to a dish, or the seeds can be removed from the pods and crushed or ground before adding. If the whole pods are added to a dish they should be removed before serving. Cardamoms are frequently used in curries and Indian cakes and desserts. In the Middle East they are used to flavour coffee. In Scandinavia, ground cardamom seed is used to flavour Danish pastries and small cakes.

Cayenne pepper – this is made from a type of dried red chilli which is ground to a powder. It has various names in different parts of the world, but is always fiery and should be used sparingly.

Chillies – these are members of the capsicum family, all of which originate from Central and South America but are now grown throughout the world. Chillies vary from mild to searing hot and come in a variety of colours from purple and yellow to the familiar bright red or green. When ripe, they are very rich in vitamin C. As a general rule, the smaller the chilli the hotter it is likely to be, whether red or green. The jalapeño chilli which features in this book is fairly hot. The hottest part of the chilli is the seeds, so these should be removed for a milder flavour. Please read the instructions in Preparing the Ingredients before handling chillies.

Cinnamon and cassia – these two spices are closely related. Both come from the inner bark of an aromatic tree related to the bay laurel. Cinnamon bark is thinner and more fragrant than the rather thicker, coarser cassia. Cassia bark is broken up and used in curries and to flavour meat stews in Greece and Cyprus. Cinnamon bark is popular in hot drinks. Ground cinnamon is probably the most widely-used sweet spice, especially in American cooking. Cinnamon, sometimes in the form of an essential oil, is also used in America to flavour many products, from toothpaste and chewing gum to Danish pastries.

Cloves – the dried, unopened bud of a member of the myrtle family has been used as a spice for thousands of years. The name comes from the French word for a nail, since this is the shape of the whole spice. Although cloves originate from the Spice Islands (the Moluccas), eighty per cent of the world's supply is now grown in Zanzibar. Cloves have been used for centuries medicinally and as breath fresheners, as well as being used whole as pickling spices. Their shape makes them handy for inserting into a vegetable or piece of meat, so that the flavour permeates the food during cooking. Hams are often dotted with cloves before boiling or baking and whole cloves are often added to stewed fruit and mulled wine. When boiling an onion, insert two whole cloves into it to add flavour. Ground cloves are used in sweet spice mixtures, often combined with ginger, for gingerbreads and honey cakes.

Coriander – this is one of the few plants which is used in its entirety in cooking. The leaves, stems and seeds all have a similar strong, sweetish aroma which adds flavour to soups and stews. The seeds are more aromatic if lightly toasted before use. Coriander is a spice that is extensively used in Asia, from the Near East to China, as well as in North Africa and Central America. It blends well with chilli and the seeds are used to flavour both Mexican chilli powder and Indian chilli mixtures. A pinch of ground coriander seed will enhance spice mixtures used in cakes, puddings and pies. Coriander is now grown under glass in Britain, largely for the ethnic food trade and it is also imported from the Netherlands.

Cumin – this pungent flavouring predominates in curries, pickles and chutneys and is the favourite spice of India. It is used whole or ground. Cumin seed, which comes from the Middle East, is used similarly to caraway in the West, as a flavouring for cheeses and breads. It is also an essential ingredient in couscous spice. Used sparingly, cumin adds interesting flavour to stews and roasts and to bland vegetables such as cauliflower. Whole cumin seeds benefit from light toasting before use to bring out the full flavour.

Fennel – There are two types of fennel, sweet fennel the herb and Florence fennel with an almost onion-shaped bulb which is used as a vegetable. In southern Europe and the Middle East it proliferates like a weed in wheatfields. Fennel originated in the Middle East and travelled eastwards to India, where the seeds are used in spice mixtures. The bulbs, stems and leaves are used extensively in Italian cooking, especially with fish and in salads. Fennel seeds (which come from both types of fennel) smell and taste strongly of aniseed and can be used like aniseed or star anise in both sweet and savoury dishes, and to flavour confectionery.

Fenugreek – these bitter seeds are used in Indian cooking though they also grow in the Near East. Fenugreek is a legume, a member of the pea family. Ground fenugreek seeds (*methi*) are used to flavour Indian spice blends, especially garam masala. They are rarely used on their own, due to their bitterness, and are usually mixed with cayenne or chilli pepper in chilli spice mixtures. Before being ground they should be lightly toasted in a dry frying pan. Fenugreek adds a subtle flavour to foods that might otherwise be cloyingly sweet, such as the nut-and-honey mixture known as halva.

Galangal (galingale or Greater galangal) – this spice was very popular in Elizabethan times but has gradually fallen out of favour in the West. It is used extensively in Thai cuisine. Galangal is related to ginger and looks similar, but the roots are less 'knobbly', and the flavour is milder and more aromatic. It is easiest to find in Oriental food shops, but if it is unavailable, substitute root ginger.

Ginger – the fat root (rhizome) of this tropical plant is used in a number of different ways. The dried root itself, also known as green ginger, is scraped, finely chopped or grated and used in curries, chutneys, pickles and other savoury dishes. The root is also boiled, then dried and ground into a fine powder. Powdered ginger is used in many traditional British cakes and puddings such as gingerbread, Yorkshire parkin, ginger nuts and ginger sponge pudding. It is also sprinkled on fresh melon. Ginger can also be preserved and made into jam or crystallised either dry or in syrup. The root is also used to flavour ginger wine. Crystallised ginger is now widely available and is delicious in fruit salads or in cakes and cake fillings.

Lemon grass – Lemon grass imparts a delicious fragrant, lemony tang to dishes. It is available fresh in larger supermarkets and Oriental food stores. Dried lemon grass is also available but has little flavour so always buy the fresh stems, whenever possible, and freeze them for future use. Lemon grass is frequently used in Thai cuisine where it is either added to a dish whole or sliced, or pounded up as an ingredient for curry paste.

Mace and *nutmeg* – nutmeg is the dried kernel of a hard nut covered in a lacy coating, called mace. Both are used as spices and although mace has a similar flavour to nutmeg, it is milder. Both nutmeg and mace are used in a wide variety of sweet and savoury dishes. Classic uses for nutmeg are as a flavouring for white sauces and custards. It tastes delicious with certain vegetables, notably cauliflower, swede and spinach. Mace is used in the same way, and whole pieces can be cooked with stewed fruit to add to the flavour.

Pepper although pepper is by far the best-known spice, there is some confusion as to the various varieties now available, and their uses. Green peppercorns are peppercorns that are in a semi-fresh state. They are used in pickling spice or coarsely ground to flavour savoury dishes. Green peppercorns are milder than the dried variety. Black pepper is particularly aromatic when freshly ground and can be mixed with, or substituted for, ginger in spice breads and honey cakes. White peppercorns are hulled peppercorns; the black skin is removed before the peppercorns have fully matured. Szechuan pepper is not a peppercorn at all, but the dried, reddish-brown berries of the prickly ash tree. It is not as hot as black pepper, however, it has a strong flavour and too much can temporarily numb the mouth. It is used in Szechuan cooking, which, unlike the rest of Chinese cuisine, is extremely hot and spicy. Hot and Sour Soup, a classic Szechuan recipe which appears in this book, is a good example.

Saffron – the most highly-prized and expensive of spices, saffron was once worth more than its weight in gold, and even today it is extremely expensive. It used to be grown commercially in Britain, mainly in East Anglia (Saffron Walden) and Cornwall, and recipes for local dishes containing saffron still survive in these areas. Saffron consists of the stigmas of the Saffron crocus. Hundreds of thousands of these bright orange strands are needed to produce one pound of the spice, which accounts for its high price. Although no longer used in medicine and as a dye, saffron is still highly-prized in cookery. Most of the saffron produced today comes from Spain and Portugal, though it is also widely grown in North Africa and Kashmir. In all of these countries it is an important ingredient in local dishes, notably rice dishes with which it has a special affinity. If saffron is unavailable or too expensive, substitute turmeric.

Star anise – this star-shaped brown fruit is widely used to impart an aniseed flavour in Chinese and Thai cuisine and is one of the ingredients in five-spice powder. It is actually no relation to the aniseed used in the West, but comes from a tree which is a member of the magnolia family. The brown pods are also chewed as a breath freshener in China. If it is unobtainable for the Thai dishes in this book, use aniseed or fennel seed instead.

Tamarind – Tamarind paste or pulp is made from the ripe bean-like fruit of the tamarind tree. It adds a fruit-sour flavour to dishes and is often used in Indian and Thai cuisine. The pulp is available in blocks from Asian and Oriental food stores. If it is unavailable substitute lemon juice.

Turmeric – the 'poor man's saffron' is widely used as a saffron substitute in Indian cooking. It is the thick root (rhizome) of a plant of the ginger family and grows widely in southern Asia. Turmeric does not have the subtlety of colour of saffron, being bright yellow rather than orange-yellow, nor the subtlety of flavour, since it is slightly bitter. It is widely used in Indian dishes of all kinds, and those of Indian origin that have become part of British cuisine, such as Mulligatawny Soup and Kedgeree, but must be used sparingly due both to its startling yellow colour and slightly bitter flavour.

Hot and Spicy Recipes

The recipes in this book provide a selection of ways in which to use hot spices. All the spices used here are obtainable in large supermarkets, but some other ingredients may be hard to find outside the big cities. Spices bought in ethnic food shops will always be fresh because there is a high turnover in these commodities, so look for them there first.

The recipes listed here include classic dishes such as Chilli con Carne and Shahi Korma, as well as new and delicious ideas for using spices such as Leg of Lamb with Chilli Sauce. Remember when serving spicy dishes to taste the mixture frequently to ensure it is to your liking; some people prefer the spicing to be subtle, others can't make them hot enough!

When serving spicy dishes to guests, always ensure there are cooling drinks on the table, to quench the thirst. Menu-planning is particularly important when the main course is strongly-flavoured, to ensure that other dishes are compatible. The fresh, fruity desserts and traditional accompaniments in this book are especially designed to go well with hot and spicy main courses.

Spicy dishes do not have to be so hot as to burn the roof off your mouth! Hopefully, this book will give you inspiration to use spices subtly to enhance or alter the flavour of dishes you already make, as well as illustrating the variety of ways in which different flavourings can improve a dish.

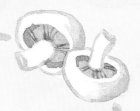

Chapter 1
Starters

BEEF AND BEAN SOUP

In Mexico, the day's main meal is eaten at
around 2.00 pm and this soup is a popular starter.

SERVES 4

1 large onion, finely chopped
2 sticks celery, chopped
1 red pepper, finely chopped
2 tbsps oil
225g/8oz minced beef
6 tomatoes, skinned, seeded and chopped
420g/15oz can refried beans
1 tsp ground cumin
1 tsp chilli powder
1 tsp crushed garlic
Pinch each of cinnamon and cayenne pepper
Salt and pepper
570ml/1 pint beef stock
Tortilla chips and soured cream to serve (optional)

1. Fry the onion, celery and pepper in the oil in a large saucepan until softened.

2. Add the beef and fry over a medium heat until well browned. Add the tomatoes and refried beans with the spices, garlic and seasoning and mix well.

3. Stir in the stock and bring to the boil. Cover and simmer gently for 30 minutes, stirring occasionally.

4. Pour the soup into a blender or food processor and purée. The soup will be quite thick, and not completely smooth.

5. Adjust the seasoning and serve with tortilla chips. Top with soured cream if wished.

Step 2 Cook the beef over a medium heat until well browned.

Step 1 Cook the onion, celery and pepper in the oil to soften. Stir frequently.

Step 4 Purée the soup in several batches until nearly smooth.

Cook's Notes

Time
Preparation takes about 20 minutes and cooking takes about 50 minutes.

Watchpoint
Make sure the blender or food processor lid is closed securely before puréeing the hot soup. Purée in 2 or 3 small batches for safety.

Freezing
Allow the puréed soup to cool completely and skim any fat from the surface. Pour into freezer containers, label and freeze for up to 3 months.

HOT & SOUR SOUP

A very warming soup, this is a favourite in winter in Peking.
Add chilli sauce and vinegar to suit your taste.
SERVES 4-6

60g/2oz lean pork
3 dried Chinese mushrooms
60g/2oz peeled, uncooked prawns
1.4 litres/2½ pints chicken stock
30g/1oz canned bamboo shoots, sliced
3 spring onions, shredded
Salt and pepper
1 tbsp sugar
1 tsp dark soy sauce
½ tsp light soy sauce
1-2 tsps chilli sauce
1½ tbsps vinegar
Dash of sesame seed oil and rice wine or sherry
1 egg, well beaten
2 tbsps water mixed with 1 tbsp cornflour

Step 2 Soak the dry mushrooms in boiling water for 5 minutes until they soften and swell. Remove the stalks before chopping.

Step 3 Pour the egg into the hot soup and stir gently to form threads.

Step 1 Cut the pork into thin shreds, long enough to fit comfortably into a soup spoon.

1. Trim any fat from the pork and slice it into shreds about 5cm/2 inches long and less than 5mm/¼ inch thick.

2. Soak the mushrooms in boiling water for 5 minutes or until softened then remove the stalks and slice the caps. Place the pork in a large pot with the prawns and stock. Bring to the boil and then reduce the heat to allow to simmer gently for 4-5 minutes. Add the bamboo shoots, spring onions, mushrooms and all the seasonings and flavourings. Cook a further 1-2 minutes over a low heat.

3. Remove the pan from the heat and gradually add the egg, stirring gently until it forms threads in the soup.

4. Mix a spoonful of the hot soup with the cornflour and water mixture and add to the soup, stirring constantly.

5. Bring the soup back to simmering point for 1 minute to thicken. Serve immediately.

Cook's Notes

Time
Preparation takes about 25 minutes, cooking takes 7-8 minutes.

Variation
Hot and Sour Soup is very versatile. Substitute other ingredients such as chicken, crabmeat, bean sprouts, spinach or green cabbage.

Watchpoint
The soup must be hot enough to cook the egg when it is added, but not so hot that the egg sets immediately.

GLASS NOODLE SOUP

This attractive soup contains spicy meatballs and, of course, the cellophane noodles which give the dish its name.

SERVES 4

2 tbsps oil
2 cloves garlic, thinly sliced
60g/2oz dried cellophane noodles
225g/8oz skinned and boned chicken breast
2 tbsps Green Curry Paste (see below)
2 tbsps fish sauce
3 tbsps cornflour
1 tbsp chopped coriander leaves
1 litre/1¾ pints chicken stock
225g/8oz bok choy, shredded
4 spring onions, cut into 2.5cm/1-inch pieces

Green Curry Paste

16 green serrano or other small chillies, chopped
3 cloves garlic, crushed
2 stems lemon grass, roughly chopped
3 spring onions, chopped
1 tsp grated fresh root ginger
1 tsp coriander seeds
1 tsp caraway seeds
4 whole cloves
1 tsp ground nutmeg
1 tsp shrimp paste
3 tbsps oil

1. First make the curry paste. Place the chillies, garlic, lemon grass and spring onions in a pestle and mortar and pound until the mixture is well bruised and the juices begin to blend.

2. Add the ginger, spices and shrimp paste and continue to pound until a paste is formed. Finally, blend in the oil.

3. To prepare the soup, heat the oil in a small frying pan or wok and fry the garlic until golden. Remove with a slotted spoon and drain on kitchen paper.

Step 5 Place the chicken, curry paste, fish sauce, cornflour and coriander into food processor and process until very finely minced.

4. Place the noodles in a large bowl and cover with hot water, allow to soak until softened, then drain.

5. Cut the chicken into chunks, place in a food processor with the 2 tbsps curry paste, fish sauce, cornflour and coriander and process until very finely minced. Remove the mixture from the processor and shape into small balls.

6. Heat the stock in a large saucepan until boiling and add the meatballs. Cook for 10-15 minutes, or until they rise to the surface.

7. Add the softened noodles, bok choy and spring onions and continue to cook for 5 minutes. Serve sprinkled with the fried garlic slices.

Step 6 Cook the meatballs for 10-15 minutes, or until they rise to the surface.

Cook's Notes

Time
Preparation takes 30 minutes and cooking takes 15-20 minutes.

Cook's Tip
Store the unused Green Curry Paste in an airtight jar in the refrigerator. It will keep for up to 1 month.

SPICY VEGETABLE FRITTERS WITH TOMATO SAUCE

This delicious dish makes an ideal starter or interesting snack.
Use any favourite vegetables or those that are in season.

SERVES 4-6

120g/4oz plain flour
120g/4oz wholemeal flour
1 tsp salt
1 tsp chilli powder
1 tsp ground cumin
280ml/½ pint water
1 tbsp lemon juice
1 small cauliflower, broken into small florets
1 aubergine, cut into 2.5cm/1-inch cubes
3 courgettes, trimmed and cut into 2.5cm/1-inch
  pieces
225g/8oz button mushrooms
1 red pepper, cut into 5mm/¼-inch thick rounds
1 green pepper, cut into 5mm/¼-inch thick rounds
1 large potato, peeled and cut into 2.5cm/1-inch cubes
400g/14oz canned plum tomatoes, drained
1 red chilli, seeded and chopped
1 clove garlic, crushed
1 small onion, finely chopped
1 tbsp white wine vinegar
1 tbsp soft brown sugar
Salt and freshly ground black pepper, to taste
1 green chilli and 1 red, sliced to garnish
Oil for deep-frying

1. Put the flours, salt, chilli powder and cumin into a large bowl. Make a slight well in the centre. Gradually add the water and lemon juice to the flour, beating well until a smooth batter is formed.

2. Wash the fresh vegetables and allow them to drain completely on kitchen paper or a clean cloth before cutting them up.

3. Put the tomatoes, fresh chilli, garlic, onion, vinegar and sugar into a food processor or liquidiser and blend until the sauce is smooth.

4. Pour the sauce mixture into a small pan and heat gently, stirring until it is completely warmed through. Season with salt and transfer to a small serving dish and garnish with slices of red and green chillies.

5. Heat some vegetable oil in a deep-fat fryer until it is warm enough to brown a 2.5cm/1-inch cube of bread in just under 1 minute.

6. Make sure the prepared vegetables are completely dry, patting any moisture off them with kitchen paper if necessary. Using a slotted spoon drop the vegetables, a few at a time, into the batter and dip them to coat thoroughly.

7. Remove the vegetables from the batter, again using the slotted spoon, and allow some of the batter to drain back into the bowl. Drop the vegetables into the hot oil, and fry quickly until they are golden brown and the batter puffy.

8. Remove the fried vegetables from the oil and drain completely on kitchen paper, keeping them warm until all the remaining vegetables have been prepared in this manner.

9. Serve immediately, providing small forks with which to dip the vegetables into the spicy tomato sauce.

Cook's Notes

Time
Preparation takes about 20 minutes, cooking takes about 30 minutes.

Watchpoint
It is important to ensure that the vegetables are completely dry before coating with the batter, or it will not cover them.

CHICKEN SATAY

This typical Indonesian dish is very spicy, and can be served
as a starter or light main course.

SERVES 4

2 tbsps soy sauce
2 tbsps sesame oil
2 tbsps lime juice
1 tsp ground cumin
1 tsp turmeric powder
2 tsps ground coriander
460g/1lb chicken breast, cut into 2.5cm/1-inch cubes
2 tbsps peanut oil
1 small onion, very finely chopped
1 tsp chilli powder
120g/4oz crunchy peanut butter
1 tsp brown sugar
Lime wedges and coriander leaves to garnish

1. Put the soy sauce, sesame oil, lime juice, cumin, turmeric and coriander into a large bowl and mix well.

2. Add the cubed chicken to the soy sauce marinade and stir well to coat the meat evenly.

3. Cover with clingfilm and allow to stand in a refrigerator for at least 1 hour, but preferably overnight.

4. Drain the meat, reserving the marinade. Thread the meat onto 4 large or 8 small skewers and set aside.

5. Heat the peanut oil in a small saucepan and add the onion and chilli powder. Cook gently until the onion is slightly softened.

6. Stir the reserved marinade into the oil and onion mixture, along with the peanut butter and brown sugar. Heat gently, stirring constantly, until all the ingredients are well blended.

7. If the sauce is too thick, stir in 2-3 tbsps boiling water.

8. Arrange the skewers of meat on a grill pan and cook under a preheated moderate grill for 10-15 minutes. After the first 5 minutes of cooking, brush the skewered meat with a little of the peanut sauce to baste.

9. During the cooking time turn the meat frequently to cook it on all sides and prevent it browning.

10. Garnish the satays with the lime and coriander leaves, and serve the remaining sauce separately.

Step 4 Thread the marinated meat onto 4 large, or 8 small, kebab skewers.

Step 8 Brush the partially grilled chicken with a little of the peanut sauce to baste.

Cook's Notes

Time
Preparation takes about 25 minutes plus at least 1 hour marinating, cooking takes about 15 minutes.

Serving Idea
Serve with a mixed salad or rice for a light lunch dish.

Preparation
The Satays may also be cooked on a barbecue.

NACHOS

These make excellent cocktail savouries and the variety of toppings and flavour combinations is almost endless.

SERVES 8-10

1 packet round tortilla chips
225g/8oz canned refried beans
1 can Jalapeño bean dip
280ml/½ pint Taco Sauce (see recipe)
8-10 cherry tomatoes, sliced
140ml/¼ pint soured cream or natural yogurt
Black and stuffed green olives, sliced
Cheddar cheese, grated

Taco Filling
2 tsps oil
225g/8oz minced beef
2 tsps chilli powder
Pinch of ground coriander
Pinch of cayenne pepper
Salt and pepper

1. Prepare the taco filling as for the Tacos recipe. Top

Step 1 Use a teaspoon to top the chips with beans and the beef mixture. Spread out carefully with the bowl of the spoon.

Step 2 Spoon on taco sauce and Jalapeño bean dip on top of beans or beef.

half of the tortilla chips with refried beans and half with the beef taco filling.

2. Place a spoonful of taco sauce on the bean-topped chips and Jalapeño bean dip in the beef-topped chips.

3. Top the tortilla chips with tomatoes, soured cream or yogurt, olives or cheese in any combination, and serve.

Step 3 Top with chosen ingredients and serve.

Cook's Notes

Time
Preparation takes about 25 minutes.

Variation
If wished, heat the Nachos through for 5 minutes in a moderate oven before topping with tomatoes, soured cream or olives. Cheese may be sprinkled on to melt before serving.

Cook's Tip
The tortilla chips will become slightly soggy if topped too soon before serving.

BARBECUED SPARERIBS

Although Chinese barbecue sauce is nothing like the tomato-based
American-style sauce, these ribs are just as tasty.

SERVES 4-6

4-6 spring onions to garnish
1.8kg/4lbs fresh pork spareribs
3 tbsps dark soy sauce
90ml/6 tbsps hoisin sauce
2 tbsps dry sherry
¼ tsp five-spice powder
1 tbsp brown sugar

1. First prepare the garnish. Trim the root ends and the dark green tops from the onions. Cut both ends into thin strips, leaving about 1.25cm/½-inch in the middle uncut.

2. Place the onions in iced water for several hours or overnight for the ends to curl up.

3. Cut the spareribs into single rib pieces. Mix all the remaining ingredients together, pour over the ribs and stir to coat evenly. Allow to stand for 1 hour.

4. Put the sparerib pieces on a rack in a roasting tin containing 570ml/1 pint water and cook in a preheated 180°C/350°F/Gas Mark 4 oven for 30 minutes. Add more hot water to the tin while cooking, if necessary.

5. Turn the ribs over and brush with the remaining sauce. Cook for 30 minutes longer, or until tender. Serve garnished with the spring onion 'brushes'.

Step 1 Cut both ends of the onions into thin strips, leaving the middle whole.

Step 1 Trim the root ends and the green tops from the onions.

Step 2 Place in iced water and leave to stand 4 hours or overnight until the ends curl.

Cook's Notes

Time
Preparation takes about 45 minutes. The onion 'brushes' must soak for at least 4-5 hours and the ribs must marinate for 1 hour. Cooking takes about 1 hour.

Preparation
If the ribs are small and not very meaty, cut into two-rib pieces before cooking, then into one-rib pieces just before serving.

Cook's Tip
The ribs may be prepared in advance and reheated at the same temperature for about 10 minutes.

VEGETABLE SAMOSAS

Samosas are a popular Indian snack that are
now available in many supermarkets.

MAKES 18

460g/1lb potatoes
2 tbsps cooking oil
½ tsp black mustard seeds
1 tsp cumin seeds
2 dried red chillies, coarsely chopped
1 medium onion, finely chopped
1-2 fresh green chillies, seeded and chopped
½ tsp ground turmeric
1 tsp ground coriander
1 tsp ground cumin
1 tsp salt or to taste
1 tbsp chopped coriander leaves
Oil for deep-frying

Pastry
225g/8oz plain flour
60g/2oz ghee or butter
½ tsp salt
75ml/2½fl oz warm water

1. Boil the potatoes in their jackets, allow to cool thoroughly, then peel and dice them.

2. Heat the oil and add mustard seeds. As soon as they start popping, add the cumin seeds and red chillies, and then the onion and green chillies. Fry till the onion is soft. Add the turmeric, coriander and cumin.

3. Add the potatoes and the salt. Reduce heat to low, stir and cook until throughly mixed. Remove from heat and add coriander leaves.

4. To make the pastry, add the ghee and salt to the flour. Rub in well. Mix a soft dough by adding the water. Knead until the dough feels soft.

5. Divide the dough into 9 pieces and roll into balls, then press them down on a work surface to make flat cakes.

6. Roll out each flat cake into 10cm/4-inch discs and cut into two. Use each semicircle of pastry as one envelope.

7. Moisten the straight edge of the pastry with a little warm water. Fold the semicircle in half to form a triangular cone. Join the straight edges by pressing them hard into each other.

8. Fill the cones with the potato mixture, leaving about 5mm/¼-inch border on the top. Moisten the top edges and press them together.

9. Heat the oil for frying to 160°C/325°F. Deep-fry only a few samosas at a time until golden brown. Drain on absorbent kitchen paper and keep warm whilst the remaining samosas are fried.

Step 9 Fill the cones, leaving about 5mm/¼-inch border on the top.

Cook's Notes

Time
Preparation takes about 1 hour.
Cooking takes about 30 minutes.

Variation
Stuff the samosas with a dry, cooked mince mixture.

SEVICHE

Do not be put off by the thought of eating raw fish, as the cod will 'cook' in the spicy marinade and the result is absolutely delicious.

SERVES 4

460g/1lb cod fillets, skinned
Grated rind and juice of 2 limes
1 shallot, chopped
1 green chilli, seeded and finely chopped
1 tsp ground coriander
1 small green pepper, sliced
1 small red pepper, sliced
1 tbsp chopped fresh parsley
1 tbsp chopped fresh coriander leaves
4 green olives, chopped
2 tbsps olive oil
Salt and pepper
1 small lettuce

Step 2 Stir the lime juice and rind, together with the shallot and spices, into the strips of cod, mixing thoroughly to coat them evenly with the spice mixture.

and rind. Add the shallot, chilli and coriander, and stir well to coat the fish completely.

3. Cover the bowl and refrigerate for 24 hours, stirring occasionally.

4. When ready to serve, drain the fish and stir in the peppers, parsley, coriander leaves, olives and oil. Season to taste and serve on a bed of lettuce.

Step 1 Cut the skinned cod fillets into thin strips across the grain, removing any bones.

Step 4 Stir the peppers, herbs, olives and oil into the drained fish.

1. Cut the cod fillets into thin strips across the grain.

2. Put the cod strips into a bowl, pour over the lime juice

Cook's Notes

Time
Preparation takes about 20 minutes, plus 24 hours refrigeration.

Variation
Substitute haddock or monkfish fillets for the cod.

Serving Ideas
Serve with crusty French bread or tortilla chips.

SESAME CHICKEN WINGS

This is an economical starter that is also good as a
cocktail snack or as a light meal with stir-fried vegetables.

SERVES 8

12 chicken wings
1 tbsp salted black beans
1 tbsp water
1 tbsp oil
2 cloves garlic, crushed
2 slices of fresh root ginger, cut into fine shreds
2 tbsps soy sauce
1½ tbsps rice wine or dry sherry
Large pinch of black pepper
1 tbsp sesame seeds
Spring onions or coriander leaves to garnish (optional)

1. Cut off and discard the chicken wing tips. Cut
between the wing joint to separate into two pieces.

2. Crush the beans and add the water. Leave to stand.

3. Heat the oil in a wok and add the garlic and ginger.
Stir briefly and add the chicken wings. Cook for about
3 minutes, stirring, until lightly browned. Add the soy
sauce and wine and cook, stirring, about 30 seconds
longer. Add the soaked black beans and pepper.

4. Cover the wok tightly and allow to simmer for about
8-10 minutes. Uncover and turn the heat to high.
Continue cooking, stirring until the liquid is almost

Step 1 Use a knife or
scissors to cut
through thick joint
and separate the
wing into two pieces.

Step 3 Stir-fry the
garlic and ginger
briefly, add the
chicken wings and
cook, stirring, until
lightly browned.

evaporated and the chicken wings are glazed with
sauce. Remove from the heat and sprinkle the sesame
seeds over. Stir to coat completely and serve. Garnish
with spring onions or coriander leaves, if wished.

Cook's Notes

Time
Preparation takes about 25
minutes, cooking takes about 13-14
minutes.

Watchpoint
Sesame seeds pop slightly as
they cook.

Cook's Tip
You can prepare the chicken
wings ahead of time and reheat them
in the oven for 10-15 minutes at
180°C/350°F/Gas Mark 4.

TACOS

Ready-made taco shells make this famous Mexican snack easy to prepare.

MAKES 12

12 taco shells

Beef Filling
1 tbsp oil
460g/1lb minced beef
1 medium onion, chopped
2 tsps ground cumin
2 tsps chilli powder
Pinch of paprika
1 clove garlic, crushed
Salt and pepper

Chicken Filling
45g/1½oz butter or margarine
1 medium onion, chopped
1 small red pepper, chopped
2 tbsps flaked almonds
340g/12oz chicken breasts, skinned and finely
    chopped
Salt and pepper
1 piece of fresh root ginger, peeled and chopped
90ml/6 tbsps milk
2 tsps cornflour
140ml/¼ pint soured cream

Toppings
Shredded lettuce
Grated cheese
Tomatoes, seeded and chopped
Chopped spring onions
Avocado slices
Soured cream
Jalapeño peppers
Taco Sauce (see recipe)

1. Heat the oil for the beef filling in a large frying pan and brown the beef and onion, breaking the meat up with a fork as it cooks. Add the spices, garlic and seasoning and cook about 20 minutes. Set aside.

2. Melt 30g/1oz of the butter for the chicken filling in a medium saucepan and add the onion. Cook slowly until softened.

3. Add the red pepper and almonds and cook slowly until the almonds are lightly browned. Stir often during cooking. Remove to a plate and set aside.

4. Melt the remaining butter in the same saucepan and cook the chicken for about 5 minutes, turning frequently. Season and return the onion mixture to the pan along with the chopped ginger.

5. Blend the milk and cornflour together and stir into the chicken mixture. Bring to the boil and stir until very thick. Mix in the soured cream and cook gently to heat through. Do not boil.

6. Heat the taco shells on a baking sheet in a preheated 180°C/350°F/Gas Mark 4 oven for 2-3 minutes. Place on the sheet with the open ends down.

7. To fill, hold a taco shell in one hand and spoon in about 1 tbsp of either beef or chicken filling. Next, add a layer of shredded lettuce, followed by a layer of grated cheese. Add choice of other toppings and finally spoon on some taco sauce.

Step 7 Hold taco shell in the palm of the hand and fill with about 1 tbsp filling.

Cook's Notes

Time
Preparation takes about 40 minutes. Cooking takes about 20 minutes for the beef filling, 15 minutes for the chicken filling and 2-3 minutes to heat the taco shells.

Cook's Tip
Placing the taco shells on their open ends when reheating keeps them from closing up and makes filling them easier.

Serving Ideas
For a buffet, place all the topping ingredients out separately for guests to help themselves and create their own combinations.

CURRY PARCELS

A tasty snack which can also be served as a starter.

MAKES 18

225g/8oz chicken breasts
2 tbsps oil
1 small onion, finely chopped
225g/8oz cooked potato, diced
1 tbsp Red Curry Paste (see recipe for Five-Spice Pork)
2 tsps sugar
18 wonton wrappers
Oil for deep-frying
Cucumber slices to garnish

Sweet and Sour Dipping Sauce
120g/4oz cucumber, finely chopped
120g/4oz carrots, finely chopped
140ml/¼ pint white wine vinegar
60g/2oz sugar
1 tsp chopped, fresh coriander

1. Mix together all the dipping sauce ingredients and set aside in a bowl.

2. Skin the chicken and chop finely. Heat the oil in a wok and stir-fry the onion and chicken for 3 minutes.

3. Stir in the potato, curry paste and sugar and fry for a few minutes. Remove the chicken mixture to a plate.

4. Place the wonton wrappers in front of you on a damp tea-towel to prevent them drying out too quickly. Spoon a little of the filling into the centre of one of the wrappers.

5. Dampen the edges with water. Pull up the edges of the pastry and pinch together, enclosing the filling. Repeat until you have used up all the filling.

6. Heat the oil for deep-frying in a clean wok and deep-fry a few parcels at a time for 3-4 minutes or until crisp and golden.

7. Drain on kitchen paper, garnish with cucumber slices and serve with the dipping sauce.

Step 4 Place the wonton wrappers on a tea-towel and spoon a little of the filling onto the centre of each wrapper.

Step 6 Deep-fry a few parcels at a time, for 3-4 minutes or until crisp and golden.

Cook's Notes

Time
Preparation takes 20 minutes and cooking takes 30 minutes.

Variation
Use pork, beef or lamb as an alternative filling for these tasty parcels.

CHICKEN TIKKA

This popular chicken dish is traditionally cooked in the Tandoor, the Indian clay oven. This recipe has been adapted for the conventional oven.

SERVES 4

460g/1lb boneless, skinned chicken breast
1 tsp salt
Juice of ½ a lemon
½ tsp tandoori colour OR a few drops of red food colouring mixed with 1 tbsp tomato purée
2 cloves garlic, coarsely chopped
1.25cm/½-inch piece fresh root ginger, peeled and chopped
2 tsps ground coriander
½ tsp ground allspice or garam masala
¼ of whole nutmeg, finely grated
½ tsp ground turmeric
150g/5oz thick-set natural yogurt
60ml/4 tbsps corn or vegetable oil
½ tsp chilli powder

1. Cut the chicken into 2.5cm/1-inch cubes. Sprinkle with ½ tsp of the salt and the lemon juice. Mix well, cover and leave for 30 minutes.

2. Put the remaining ingredients into a liquidiser or food processor and blend until smooth.

3. Sieve the puréed mixture over the chicken pieces, using the back of a metal spoon to push it through, until only a very coarse mixture is left in the sieve.

4. Coat the chicken thoroughly with the sieved marinade. Cover and leave to marinate for 6-8 hours or overnight in the refrigerator.

5. Preheat an oven to 230°C/450°F/Gas Mark 8, and line a roasting tin with foil. Remove the chicken from the marinade and thread the pieces onto skewers, leaving 5mm/¼-inch gap between each piece.

Step 5 Thread the chicken onto skewers leaving 5mm/¼-inch gap between each piece.

6. Place the skewers in the prepared roasting tin and brush with some of the remaining marinade. Cook in the preheated oven for 6-8 minutes.

7. Remove from the oven, turn the skewers over and brush the pieces of chicken with the remaining marinade. Return to the oven and cook for a further 6-8 minutes.

8. Shake off any excess liquid from the chicken. Place the skewers on a serving dish.

Cook's Notes

Time
Preparation takes 30-35 minutes plus 6-8 hours marinating. Cooking takes 12-16 minutes.

Cook's Tip
Serve with a side salad and Indian bread to make a lunch or supper dish.

Watchpoint
Do not overcook the chicken or it will dry out.

Chapter 2

Main Courses

Kung Pao Prawns with Cashew Nuts • Blackened Fish • Fish Bhoona

Coconut Fried Fish with Chillies • Steamed Fish in Banana Leaves

Seafood Filé Gumbo • Caribbean Prawns and Sweet Potatoes in Coconut Sauce

Fish Shahjahani • Szechuan Fish • Plaice with Spicy Tomato Sauce

Prawns Veracruz • Cod Curry • New Orleans Jambalaya

Tamarind Chicken Satay • Curried Chicken Kebabs with Cucumber Sauce

Chicken Jambalaya • Country Captain Chicken • Flautas

Aubergine and Chicken Chilli • Chicken Moghlai with Coriander Chutney

Chicken Gumbo • Coriander Chicken • Chicken Tomato • Mexican Kebabs

Szechuan Meatballs • Southwestern Stir-Fry • Five-Spice Pork • Enchiladas

Chilli Beef Stew • Meat Madras • Leg of Lamb with Chilli Sauce

Mussaman Curry • Beef with Tomato and Pepper in Black Bean Sauce

Chilli con Carne • Pork with Lime and Chilli • Albondigas • Spiced Beef

Spareribs in Chilli & Cream Sauce • Shahi Korma • Chilli Verde

Shredded Beef with Vegetables • Minute Steaks with Taco Sauce

KUNG PAO PRAWNS WITH CASHEW NUTS

It is said that King Pao invented this dish, but to this day no-one seems to know who the creator of this recipe actually was!

SERVES 6

½ tsp chopped fresh ginger
1 tsp chopped garlic
1½ tbsps cornflour
¼ tsp bicarbonate of soda
Salt and pepper
¼ tsp sugar
460g/1lb uncooked, peeled prawns
60ml/4 tbsps oil
1 small onion, diced
1 large or 2 small courgettes, cut into 1.25cm/½-inch
   cubes
1 small red pepper, cut into 1.25cm/½-inch cubes
60g/2oz cashew nuts

Sauce
175ml/6 fl oz chicken stock
1 tbsp cornflour
2 tsps chilli sauce
2 tsps bean paste (optional)
2 tsps sesame oil
1 tbsp dry sherry or rice wine

To dice the courgettes quickly, top and tail and cut into 1.25cm/½-inch strips.

Cut the strips across with a large sharp knife into 1.25cm/½-inch pieces.

1. Mix together the ginger, garlic, cornflour, bicarbonate of soda, salt and pepper and sugar.

2. Remove the dark vein running along the rounded side of the prawns. If the prawns are large, cut in half. Place in the dry ingredients, turn to coat, and leave to stand for 20 minutes.

3. Heat the oil in a wok and when hot add the prawns. Cook, stirring over high heat for about 20 seconds, or just until the prawns change colour. Transfer to a plate.

4. Add the onion to the same oil in the wok and cook for about 1 minute. Add the courgettes and red pepper and cook for about 30 seconds.

5. Mix the sauce ingredients together and add to the wok. Cook, stirring constantly, until the sauce is slightly thickened. Add the prawns and the cashew nuts and heat through completely.

Cook's Notes

Time
Preparation takes about 20 minutes, cooking takes about 3 minutes.

Variation
If using cooked prawns, add at the end of cooking time with the vegetables. Vary amount of chilli sauce to suit your taste.

Serving Ideas
Serve with plain or fried rice.

BLACKENED FISH

This Cajun recipe from America has many variations for the spice mixture.
Local cooks, however, do agree that the fish should have a very
brown crust when properly blackened.

SERVES 4

225g/8oz unsalted butter
4 fish steaks or fillets, about 225g/8oz each
1 tbsp paprika
1 tsp crushed garlic
1 tsp cayenne pepper
½ tsp ground white pepper
2 tsps salt
1 tsp dried thyme

1. Melt the butter and pour about half into each of four ramekin dishes and set aside.

2. Brush each fish steak liberally with the remaining butter on both sides.

3. Mix together the spices, seasonings and thyme and sprinkle generously on each side of the steaks, patting it on by hand.

4. Heat a large, heavy-based frying pan and add about 1 tbsp butter per fish steak. When the butter is hot, add the fish (skin side down first if using fillets).

5. Turn the fish over when the underside is very brown and repeat with the remaining side. Add more butter as necessary during cooking.

6. When the top side of the fish is very dark brown, repeat with the remaining fish fillets, keeping them warm while cooking the rest.

7. Serve the fish immediately with the dishes of butter for dipping.

Step 2 Use a pastry brush to coat the fish well on both sides with the melted butter.

Step 3 Mix the seasoning ingredients together well and press firmly onto both sides of the fish to coat.

Step 5 Cook the underside and topside of the fish until very dark.

Cook's Notes

Time
Preparation takes about 20 minutes and cooking takes about 2-3 minutes per side for each steak or fillet.

Variation
Use whatever varieties of fish steaks or fillets you like but make sure they are about 2cm/¾-inch thick.

Preparation
The fish should be very dark brown on the top and the bottom before serving. Leave at least 2 minutes before attempting to turn the fish over.

FISH BHOONA

For a successful bhoona the spices must be fried
until they are a rich brown colour.

SERVES 4

680g/1½lbs steak or fillets of any white fish
90ml/6 tbsps cooking oil

Seasoned flour mixture
1 tbsp plain flour
¼ tsp ground turmeric
¼ tsp chilli powder
¼ tsp salt

1 large onion, coarsely chopped
½-inch piece fresh root ginger, peeled and chopped
2-4 cloves garlic, coarsely chopped
½ tsp ground turmeric
¼ tsp chilli powder
1 tsp ground coriander
½ tsp garam masala
1 small can tomatoes
150ml/¼ pint warm water
120g/4oz frozen garden peas
1 tsp salt
1 tbsp chopped coriander leaves

1. Skin the fish, wash and dry thoroughly and cut into 2.5 x 5cm/1 2-inch pieces, removing any bone.

2. Heat 2 tbsps of the oil in a large frying pan, preferably non-stick, over a medium heat.

3. Lightly dust the fish in the seasoned flour mixture and

Step 1 Cut the fish into 2.5 x 5cm/1 x 2-inch pieces.

place in the hot oil. Fry the fish until all the pieces are evenly browned. Drain on absorbent kitchen paper.

4. Put the onion, ginger and garlic into a liquidiser and blend until smooth.

5. Heat the remaining oil over medium heat, add the onion mixture and stir. Heat through, then turn heat down and fry for 3-4 minutes.

6. Add the turmeric, chilli, coriander and garam masala and fry for 4-5 minutes, stirring continuously. During this time add 1 tbsp juice from the tomatoes at a time to prevent the spices from sticking to the pan.

7. Now add one tomato at a time, along with any remaining juice. Cook until the tomato is well incorporated into the rest of the ingredients.

8. Add the water, peas and salt. Bring to the boil and add the fish. Cover and simmer for 5 minutes, then remove from heat. Garnish with chopped coriander.

Cook's Notes

Time
Preparation takes 15-20 minutes and cooking takes 30-35 minutes.

Cook's Tip
Use a firm white fish such as cod or monkfish for this recipe.

COCONUT FRIED FISH WITH CHILLIES

The spicy, chilli-laced tomato sauce in this recipe makes the perfect partner to the coconut coating on the fish.

SERVES 4

Oil for frying
460g/1lb sole or plaice fillets, skinned, boned and cut into 2.5cm/1-inch strips
Seasoned flour
1 egg, beaten
60g/2oz desiccated coconut
1 tbsp vegetable oil
1 tsp grated fresh root ginger
1 red chilli, seeded and finely chopped
¼ tsp chilli powder
1 tsp ground coriander
½ tsp ground nutmeg
1 clove garlic, crushed
2 tbsps tomato purée
2 tbsps tomato chutney
2 tbsps dark soy sauce
2 tbsps lemon juice
2 tbsps water
1 tsp brown sugar
Salt and pepper

Step 1 Toss the strips of fish in the flour and then dip them in the beaten egg. Roll them finally in the desiccated coconut.

Step 2 Fry the fish in the hot oil, a few pieces at a time, to prevent it from breaking up.

1. In a frying pan, heat about 5cm/2 inches of oil to 190°C/375°F. Toss the fish strips in the seasoned flour and then dip them into the beaten egg. Roll them in the desiccated coconut and shake off the excess.

2. Fry the fish, a few pieces at a time, in the hot oil and drain them on absorbent kitchen paper. Keep warm.

3. Heat the 1 tbsp oil in a wok or frying pan and fry the ginger, red chilli, spices and garlic, for about 2 minutes.

4. Add the remaining ingredients and simmer for about 3 minutes. Serve the fish, with the sauce handed round separately.

Cook's Notes

Time
Preparation takes about 30 minutes, and cooking takes about 30.

Cook's Tip
Great care should be taken when preparing fresh chillies. Always wash your hands thoroughly afterwards, and avoid getting any neat juice in your eyes or mouth. Rinse with copious amounts of clear water, if you do.

Variation
Substitute a firm-fleshed fish like haddock, or monkfish, for the plaice.

Serving Ideas
Serve with plain boiled rice, a cucumber relish and plenty of salad.

STEAMED FISH IN BANANA LEAVES (HAW MOK)

Lining the steamer with banana leaves, as they do in Thailand, imparts extra flavour to the dish, but you can use baking parchment or foil instead.

SERVES 4

460g/1lb white fish fillets, skinned
Banana leaves (optional)
2 carrots, peeled and cut into thin sticks
1 red pepper, cut into strips
120g/4oz long beans or French beans, cut into 7.5cm/3-inch lengths
2 courgettes, cut into thin sticks
140ml/¼ pint thick coconut milk
1-2 tbsps Red Curry Paste (see recipe for Five-Spice Pork)
2 kaffir lime leaves
1 tbsp fish sauce

Step 2 Line a heat-proof dish, which will fit into your steamer, with banana leaves.

Step 1 Cut the fish into bite-size pieces or strips about 1.25cm/½-inch wide.

Step 4 Pile the fish pieces on top of the vegetables in the steamer.

1. Cut the fish into bite-size pieces or strips about 1.25cm/½ inch wide.

2. Line a heatproof dish, which will fit into your steamer, with banana leaves, baking parchment or foil.

3. Blanch the carrots, pepper and beans for 2 minutes in boiling water, add the courgettes for 30 seconds then drain and scatter over the banana leaf.

4. Pile the fish on top of the vegetables.

5. Combine the remaining ingredients and pour over the fish. Cover the steamer and steam 15-20 minutes or until the fish is cooked through and flakes easily.

Cook's Notes

Time
Preparation takes 15 minutes and cooking takes about 20 minutes.

Cook's Tip
Use a firm-fleshed fish so that it won't break up during cooking.

SEAFOOD FILÉ GUMBO

Cajun filé gumbo gets its name from the use of filé powder –
a thickening agent made from the dried aromatic leaves of the
sassafras tree, a relative of the bay tree.

SERVES 8

460g/1lb cooked, unpeeled prawns
½ tbsp each of whole cloves, whole allspice, coriander
    seeds and mustard seeds
1.14 litres/2 pints water
60g/2oz butter
1 onion, sliced
1 green pepper, sliced
2 cloves garlic, finely chopped
3 tbsps flour
Sprig of thyme
1 bay leaf
2 tbsps chopped parsley
Dash of Worcestershire sauce
12 fresh oysters, on the half shell
225g/8oz tomatoes, skinned and chopped
2 tbsps filé powder (optional)
Salt and pepper
Cooked rice, to serve

Step 1 Peel the prawns, adding the heads, tail shell, legs and roe, if present, to the spice mixture in a large stock pot.

Step 3 Loosen the oysters from their shells and add to the hot mix. If wished, strain the oyster liquid through a fine mesh sieve.

1. Peel the prawns and reserve the shells. Mix the prawn shells with the spice mixture and water and bring to the boil in a large stock pot. Reduce the heat and allow to simmer for about 20 minutes.

2. Melt the butter and, when foaming, add the onion, green pepper, garlic and flour. Cook slowly, stirring constantly, until the flour is a pale golden brown. Gradually strain on the stock, discarding the shells and spice mixture. Add the thyme and bay leaf and stir well. Bring to the boil and then simmer until thick.

3. Add the parsley and the Worcestershire sauce to taste. Add the oysters, peeled prawns and tomatoes and heat through gently to cook the oysters.

4. Stir in the filé powder and leave to stand to thicken. Adjust the seasoning and serve over hot rice.

Cook's Notes

Time
Preparation takes about 25-30 minutes and cooking takes about 20-25 minutes.

Variation
If they are available, use raw, unpeeled prawns and cook with the water and the spice mixture until they turn pink and curl up. Drain them, reserving the liquid. Peel and return the shells to the stock. Re-boil the stock and allow to simmer for about 15 minutes.

Cook's Tip
If filé powder is not available, use equal portions of butter and flour mixed together to a paste. Add a bit of the paste at a time to the mix, and boil in between additions, whisking well, until the required thickness is reached.

CARIBBEAN PRAWNS AND SWEET POTATOES IN COCONUT SAUCE

Sweet potatoes are now widely available in most supermarkets
and this recipe makes delicious use of them.

SERVES 6

460g/1lb sweet potatoes, peeled and diced
1 large onion, chopped
1 clove garlic, crushed
2.5cm/1-inch piece of fresh root ginger, grated
1 red or green chilli, seeded and chopped
¼ tsp ground cumin
¼ tsp ground coriander
¼ tsp ground allspice
2 tbsps coconut cream, OR 15g/½oz creamed
    coconut, dissolved in 2 tbsps boiling water
570ml/1 pint water
120g/4oz peeled prawns
120g/4oz chicory, shredded
225g/8oz Chinese leaves, shredded
1 tbsp dark, soft brown sugar
2 tbsps lime juice
Salt
Desiccated coconut to garnish

1. In a large saucepan, mix together the sweet potatoes, onion, garlic, ginger, chilli, spices, coconut, cream and water.

2. Bring to the boil and simmer until the potato is almost tender.

3. Add the prawns, chicory and Chinese leaves. Simmer for 4-5 minutes, until the ingredients are heated through, but the leaves are still crisp.

4. Add the sugar and lime juice and season to taste. Serve sprinkled with the desiccated coconut.

Step 1 Mix together the sweet potaotes and the onion, garlic, ginger, chilli, spices, coconut cream and water in a large pan.

Step 3 Simmer the chicory and Chinese leaves with the prawns and potatoes, until they are heated through but still crisp.

Cook's Notes

Time
Preparation takes about 20 minutes, and cooking takes 20-30 minutes.

Serving Ideas
Serve with boiled rice, mixed with cooked peas and sweetcorn.

Variation
Yams can be used in this recipe instead of sweet potatoes.

Watchpoint
Great care must be taken when using fresh chillies. Do not get the juice into the eyes or mouth. If this should happen, rinse with lots of cold water.

FISH SHAHJAHANI

This rich but easy to prepare fish dish is named after the Mughal Emperor
Shahjahan, who was noted for his love of good food.

SERVES 4

680g/1½lbs fillet of any white fish
90g/3oz roasted cashews
120ml/4fl oz single cream
60g/2oz unsalted butter
225g/8oz onions, finely sliced
5cm/2-inch piece of cinnamon stick, broken up
4 green cardamoms, split open the top of each pod
2 whole cloves
1-2 fresh green chillies, sliced lengthways
1 tsp ground turmeric
175ml/6fl oz warm water
1 tsp salt
1 tbsp lemon juice

1. Rinse the fish gently in cold water, dry on absorbent kitchen paper and cut into 2.5 x 5cm/1 x 2-inch pieces.

2. Put the cashews and the cream in a liquidiser or food processor and blend to a reasonably fine mixture.

3. In a wide, shallow pan melt the butter over medium heat and fry onions, cinnamon, cardamom, cloves and green chillies until the onions are lightly browned. Stir in the turmeric.

4. Add the water and salt and add the fish in a single layer. Bring to the boil, cover the pan and simmer for 2-3 minutes.

5. Now add the cashew and cream mixture and stir gently until the pieces of fish are well coated. Cover the pan again and simmer for a further 2-3 minutes.

6. Remove from heat and gently stir in the lemon juice. Remove cinnamon pieces and cardamoms before serving.

Step 3 Fry the onions, spices and chillies until the onions are lightly browned.

Step 5 Add the cashew and cream mixture and stir gently until the pieces of fish are well coated.

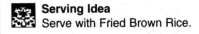

Cook's Notes

Time
Preparation takes 15 minutes and cooking takes 15-20 minutes.

Watchpoint
It is important to use a wide shallow pan so that the fish can be arranged in a single layer to prevent it from breaking up during cooking.

Serving Idea
Serve with Fried Brown Rice.

SZECHUAN FISH

The piquant spiciness of Szechuan pepper is quite different from that of black or white pepper. Beware, though, too much can numb the mouth temporarily!

SERVES 6

Fresh red or green chillies to garnish
460g/1lb white fish fillets
Pinch of salt and pepper
1 egg
38g/5 tbsps flour
90ml/6 tbsps white wine
Oil for frying
60g/2oz cooked ham, cut in small dice
2.5cm/1-inch piece fresh root ginger, finely diced
½-1 red or green chilli, seeded and finely diced
6 water chestnuts, finely diced
4 spring onions, finely chopped
3 tbsps light soy sauce
1 tsp cider vinegar or rice wine vinegar
½ tsp ground Szechuan pepper
280ml/½ pint light stock
1 tbsp cornflour blended with 2 tbsps water
2 tsps sugar

Step 1 Cut the tip of each chilli into strips.

1. To prepare the garnish, choose unblemished chillies with the stems on. Using a small, sharp knife, cut them in strips, starting from the pointed end.

2. Cut down to within 1.25cm/½ inch of the stem end. Rinse out the seeds under cold running water and place them in iced water.

3. Leave the chillies to soak for at least 4 hours or overnight until they open up like flowers.

4. Cut the fish fillets into 5cm/2 inch pieces and season with salt and pepper. Beat the egg well and add the flour and wine to make a batter.

5. Heat a wok and when hot, add enough oil to deep-fry the fish. When the oil is hot, dredge the fish lightly with flour and then dip into the batter. Mix the fish well. Fry a few pieces of fish at a time, until golden brown. Drain and proceed until all the fish is cooked.

6. Remove all but 1 tbsp of oil from the wok and add the ham, ginger, diced chilli, water chestnuts and spring onions. Cook for about 1 minute and add the soy sauce, vinegar and Szechuan pepper. Stir well and cook for a further 1 minute. Remove the vegetables from the pan and set them aside.

7. Add the stock to the wok and bring to the boil. When boiling, add a spoonful of the hot stock to the cornflour mixture. Add the mixture back to the stock and reboil, stirring constantly until thickened.

8. Stir in the sugar and add the fish and vegetables to the sauce. Heat through for 30 seconds and serve at once.

Cook's Notes

Time
Preparation takes about 30 minutes. Chilli garnish takes at least 4 hours to soak. Cooking takes about 10 minutes.

Buying Guide
Szechuan peppercorns are available in Chinese supermarkets or delicatessens. If not available, substitute extra chillies.

Serving Ideas
Serve with plain or fried rice.

PLAICE WITH SPICY TOMATO SAUCE

This piquant fish dish is popular along Mexico's Gulf coast.

SERVES 4

90g/3oz cream cheese
1 tsp dried oregano
Pinch of cayenne pepper
4 whole fillets of plaice
Lime slices and dill to garnish

Tomato Sauce
1 tbsp oil
1 small onion, chopped
1 stick celery, chopped
1 chilli, seeded and chopped
¼ tsp each of ground cumin, coriander and ginger
½ red and ½ green pepper, chopped
400g/14oz can tomatoes
1 tbsp tomato purée
Salt, pepper and a pinch of sugar

1. Heat the oil for the tomato sauce in a heavy-based pan and cook the onion, celery, chilli and spices for about 5 minutes over a very low heat.

2. Add the red and green peppers and the remaining sauce ingredients and bring to the boil. Reduce heat and simmer for 15-20 minutes, stirring occasionally. Set aside while preparing the fish.

3. Mix the cream cheese, oregano and cayenne pepper together and set aside.

4. Skin the plaice fillets using a filleting knife. Start at the tail end and hold the knife at a slight angle to the skin. Push the knife along using a sawing motion, with the blade against the skin. Dip your fingers in salt to make it easier to hold onto the fish skin. Gradually separate the fish from the skin.

5. Spread the cheese filling on all 4 fillets and roll each up. Secure with cocktail sticks.

6. Place the fillets in a lightly greased baking dish, cover and cook in an oven preheated to 180°C/350°F/Gas Mark 4 for 10 minutes.

7. Pour over the tomato sauce and cook for a further 10-15 minutes. The fish is cooked when it feels firm and looks opaque. Garnish with lime slices and dill.

Step 4 Using a filleting knife held at an angle, push the knife along, cutting against the fish skin. Use a sawing motion to separate flesh from skin.

Step 5 Spread cheese filling on the fish and roll up each fillet.

Cook's Notes

Time
Preparation takes about 30 minutes and cooking takes 20-25 minutes.

Serving Ideas
Serve with rice and an avocado salad.

Variation
Add prawns or crabmeat to the filling for a dinner party.

PRAWNS VERACRUZ

Veracruz is a port on the Gulf of Mexico which lends its name to a variety of colourful seafood dishes.

SERVES 4

1 tbsp oil
1 onion, chopped
1 large green pepper, cut into 3.5cm/1½-inch strips
2-3 green chillies, seeded and chopped
570ml/1 pint Taco Sauce (see recipe)
2 tomatoes, skinned and roughly chopped
12 pimento-stuffed olives, halved
2 tsps capers
¼ tsp ground cumin
Salt
460g/1lb uncooked prawns, peeled
Juice of 1 lime

1. Heat the oil in a large frying pan and add the onion and green pepper. Cook until soft but not coloured.

2. Add the chillies, taco sauce, tomatoes, olives, capers, cumin and some salt to taste. Bring to the boil

To skin the tomatoes, place them in a pan of boiling water for a few seconds.

Refresh the blanched tomatoes in cold water. The skins will now peel away easily.

Step 2 Combine all the sauce ingredients in a heavy-based pan.

and then lower the heat to simmer for 5 minutes.

3. Remove black veins, if present, from the rounded side of the prawns with a cocktail stick.

4. Add the prawns to the sauce and cook for about 5 minutes or until they curl up and turn pink and opaque. Add the lime juice to taste and serve.

Cook's Notes

Time
Preparation takes about 25 minutes and cooking takes about 15 minutes.

Preparation
The sauce may be prepared in advance and reheated while cooking the prawns.

Variation
If using cooked prawns, reheat for about 5 minutes. Do not overcook.

COD CURRY

The fragrant spices used in this recipe are now
readily available at most supermarkets.

SERVES 4

1 large onion, chopped
3 tbsps vegetable oil
2.5cm/1-inch piece cinnamon stick
1 bay leaf
1 tsp ginger paste
1 tsp garlic paste
1 tsp chilli powder
1 tsp ground cumin
1 tsp ground coriander
¼ tsp ground turmeric
140ml/¼ pint natural yogurt OR 225g/8oz canned
    tomatoes, chopped
1-2 fresh green chillies, chopped
2 sprigs fresh coriander leaves, chopped
460g/1lb cod cutlets, or fillets, cut into 5cm/2-inch
    pieces
1 tsp salt

1. In a large heavy-based frying pan, fry the onion in the
oil until golden brown. Add the cinnamon, bay leaf and
the ginger and garlic pastes and fry for 1 minute.

2. Add the ground spices and fry for a further minute,
then stir in either the yogurt, or the tomatoes and the
chopped chillies and coriander leaves.

Step 1 Fry the
cinnamon, bay leaf
and the ginger and
garlic pastes with the
onion for 1 minute.

3. Only if you have used yogurt, stir in 140ml/¼ pint
water and simmer the mixture for 2-3 minutes. Do not
add any water if you have used the tomatoes.

4. Stir the cod into the sauce, and add the salt. Cover
the pan and simmer for 15-18 minutes before serving.

Step 4 Add the cod
pieces to the sauce
in the pan, stir well to
coat thoroughly
before covering and
simmer for 15-18
minutes.

Cook's Notes

Time
Preparation takes about 15
minutes, and cooking takes about 20
minutes.

Cook's Tip
Great care should be taken when
preparing fresh chillies. Always wash
hands thoroughly afterwards. For a
milder curry, remove the seeds; for a
hotter curry, leave them in.

Serving Ideas
Serve with boiled rice and a
cucumber raita.

NEW ORLEANS JAMBALAYA

There are countless versions of this spicy soup-stew. Its origins have been likened to the Spanish dish Paella.

SERVES 4-6

30g/1oz butter or margarine
2 tbsps flour
1 medium onion, finely chopped
1 clove garlic, crushed
1 red pepper, finely chopped
400g/14oz can tomatoes
1.14 litres/2 pints fish or chicken stock
¼ tsp ground ginger
Pinch of allspice
1 tsp chopped fresh thyme or ½ tsp dried thyme
¼ tsp cayenne pepper
Pinch of salt
Dash of Tabasco
120g/4oz uncooked rice
900g/2lbs uncooked prawns, peeled
2 spring onions, chopped to garnish

Step 1 Cook the flour and butter roux until it is a pale straw colour.

Step 3 Add the uncooked rice directly into the sauce and stir well.

1. Melt the butter in a heavy-based saucepan and then add the flour. Stir to blend well and cook over low heat until a pale straw colour. Add the onion, garlic and pepper and cook until soft.

2. Add the tomatoes and their juice, breaking up the tomatoes with a fork or a potato masher. Add the stock and mix well. Add the ginger, allspice, thyme, cayenne pepper, salt and Tabasco. Bring to the boil and allow to boil rapidly, stirring for about 2 minutes.

3. Add the rice, stir well and cover the pan. Cook for about 12-15 minutes, or until the rice is tender and has absorbed most of the liquid.

4. Add the prawns during the last 10 minutes of cooking time. Cook until the prawns curl and turn pink. Adjust the seasoning, spoon into a serving dish and sprinkle with the chopped spring onion to serve.

Cook's Notes

Time
Preparation takes about 40 minutes and cooking takes about 25-30 minutes.

Cook's Tip
If the rice still has a lot of liquid left before adding the prawns, uncover and boil rapidly, stirring once or twice, for about 5 minutes. This should evaporate the excess liquid.

Variation
If wished, use fresh tomatoes, skinned, seeded and chopped. Add about 90ml/3fl oz extra stock. Green pepper may be used instead of red pepper, if preferred.

TAMARIND CHICKEN SATAY

Traditionally satay is served as only a part of a meal, but this version is so good that it needs only a tomato sambal as an accompaniment.

SERVES 4

4 chicken breasts, skinned, boned and cut into
   2.5cm/1-inch cubes

Marinade
1 tbsp oil
5cm/2-inch piece tamarind, soaked in 100ml/4fl oz hot
   water or lemon juice
2 cloves garlic, crushed
1 tsp ground cardamom
½ tsp ground nutmeg
Salt and pepper
1 tsp kecap manis (sweet soy sauce)

Tomato and Chilli Sambal
2 red chillies
1 small piece fresh root ginger, grated
1 clove garlic, crushed
460g/1lb fresh tomatoes, skinned and seeded
60ml/4 tbsps oil
1 tbsp lemon or lime juice
1 tbsp dark brown sugar
Salt and pepper

Step 1 Put the chicken and marinade into a large bowl and stir to coat thoroughly.

Step 5 Cook the chicken skewers under a preheated grill. Use a brush to baste them with the remaining marinade as they cook.

1. Put the chicken cubes in a large bowl. Mix together the marinade ingredients and pour them over the chicken. Stir well and refrigerate for at least 30 minutes.

2. To prepare the sambal, grind together the chillies, ginger and garlic in a food processor, or pound using a pestle and mortar. Chop the tomatoes coarsely and blend them into the chilli mixture.

3. Heat the oil in a wok or large frying pan and fry the tomato mixture for about 5-6 minutes, stirring occasionally to prevent it sticking. Add the lemon juice and a spoonful of water, if the sauce becomes too thick. Stir in the sugar and seasoning to taste.

4. Remove the chicken from the marinade and thread onto thin wooden skewers. Place on a grill pan.

5. Cook the chicken under a preheated grill for 8-10 minutes, turning frequently, until golden brown. Brush the chicken with the remaining marinade during cooking.

Cook's Notes

Time
Preparation takes about 15 minutes plus 30 minutes marinating. Cooking takes 10-15 minutes.

Serving Ideas
Serve the satay on a bed of rice with the tomato and chilli sambal.

Cook's Tip
If you cannot obtain tamarind use the juice of 2 lemons instead. The kecap manis may be hard to find and can be replaced by ½ tsp dark brown sugar and 1 tsp dark soy sauce.

Preparation
The chicken satays can be cooked very successfully on an outdoor barbecue grill.

CURRIED CHICKEN KEBABS WITH CUCUMBER SAUCE

This dish makes a colourful and spicy main course.
Cucumber in yogurt makes a cooling accompaniment.

SERVES 4

3 chicken breasts, skinned and boned

Marinade
2 tbsps vegetable oil
1 clove garlic, crushed
2 tsps curry powder
¼ tsp cayenne pepper
1 tbsp chopped coriander leaves
Grated rind and juice of 1 lime
Salt and pepper

Sauce
½ cucumber, grated
280ml/½ pint nautral yogurt
1 tbsp chopped fresh mint
1 tsp mango chutney
Pinch of salt and pepper

1. Cut the chicken into 2.5cm/1-inch cubes. Combine the ingredients for the marinade and mix with the chicken to coat each piece. Leave to marinate for 1 hour.

2. While the chicken is marinating, sprinkle the grated cucumber lightly with salt and leave to stand.

3. Rinse thoroughly and pat dry with absorbent kitchen

Step 1 Cut the chicken into cubes and combine them with the marinade, coating each piece thoroughly.

paper. Combine with the remaining sauce ingredients.

4. Thread the chicken onto wooden skewers and place on a grill pan. Cook under a preheated grill for 10-12 minutes, turning the kebabs frequently while cooking. Serve with the cucumber and yogurt sauce.

Step 4 Thread the marinaded chicken strips onto wooden skewers.

Cook's Notes

Time
Preparation takes about 10 minutes, plus 1 hour to marinate the chicken. Cooking takes 10-12 minutes.

Variation
Other herbs and spices may be added to the marinade.

Economy
The recipe can be prepared with meat from drumsticks or thighs. Add about 1 minute to the cooking time.

CHICKEN JAMBALAYA

Jambalaya is a hearty one-pot meal which can be made with whatever ingredients you have to hand.

SERVES 4-6

1.4kg/3lbs chicken portions, skinned, boned, and cut
   into cubes
1 large onion, roughly chopped
3 sticks celery, roughly chopped
45g/1½oz butter or margarine
1 large green pepper, roughly chopped
1 clove garlic, crushed
1 tsp each of cayenne, white and black pepper
225g/8oz uncooked rice
400g/14oz can tomatoes
175g/6oz smoked sausage, cut into 1.25cm/½-inch
   dice
850ml/1½ pints chicken stock
Chopped parsley

Step 1 Put the skin and bones in a large stock pot with the onion and celery trimmings to make the stock. Add water to cover.

Step 1 Remove the skin from the chicken and set aside.

1. Use the chicken skin, and the onion and celery trimmings to make stock. Cover the ingredients with water, bring to the boil and then simmer slowly for 1 hour. Strain and reserve.

2. Melt the butter or margarine in a large saucepan and add the onion. Cook slowly to brown and then add the celery, green pepper and garlic and cook briefly.

3. Add the three kinds of pepper and the rice, stirring to mix well.

4. Add the chicken, tomatoes, sausage and stock and mix well. Bring to the boil, then simmer for about 20-25 minutes, stirring occasionally, until the chicken is done and the rice is tender. The rice should have absorbed most of the liquid by the time it has cooked. Garnish with chopped parsley before serving.

Cook's Notes

Time
Preparation takes about 35-40 minutes and cooking takes about 20-25 minutes.

Preparation
Check the level of liquid occasionally as the rice is cooking and add more water or stock as necessary. If there is a lot of liquid left and the rice is nearly cooked, uncover the pan and boil rapidly.

Serving Ideas
Add a green salad to make a complete meal.

COUNTRY CAPTAIN CHICKEN

A flavourful dish named after a sea captain with a
taste for the spicy cuisine of India.

SERVES 6

1.4kg/3lbs chicken portions, skinned
Seasoned flour
90ml/6 tbsps oil
1 medium onion, chopped
1 medium green pepper, chopped
1 clove garlic, crushed
Pinch of salt and pepper
2 tsps curry powder
2 x 400g/14oz cans tomatoes
2 tsps chopped fresh parsley
1 tsp chopped fresh marjoram
45g/4 tbsps currants or raisins
120g/4oz blanched almond halves

1. Dredge the chicken with flour, shaking off the excess.

2. Heat the oil in a large frying pan and brown the chicken on all sides until golden. Remove to an ovenproof casserole.

3. Pour off all but 2 tbsps of the oil. Add the onion, pepper and garlic and cook slowly to soften.

4. Add the seasoning and curry powder and cook, stirring frequently, for 2 minutes. Add the tomatoes, parsley and marjoram and bring to the boil. Pour the sauce over the chicken, cover and cook in an oven preheated to 180°C/350°F/Gas Mark 4, for 45 minutes. Add the currants or raisins during the last 15 minutes.

5. Meanwhile, toast the almonds in the oven on a baking sheet alongside the chicken. Stir them frequently and watch carefully. Sprinkle over the chicken just before serving.

Step 4 Add the curry powder to the vegetables in the frying pan and cook for 2 minutes over low heat stirring frequently.

Step 4 Cook the sauce ingredients and pour over the chicken.

Step 5 Toast the almonds on a baking sheet in the oven until light golden brown.

Cook's Notes

Time
Preparation takes about 30 minutes and cooking takes about 50 minutes.

Preparation
Country Captain Chicken can be prepared completely ahead of time and reheated for about 20 minutes in a moderate oven.

Serving Idea
If wished, serve the chicken with an accompaniment of boiled rice.

FLAUTAS

Traditionally, these are long, thin rolls of tortillas with
savoury fillings, topped with soured cream.

SERVES 6

225g/8oz chicken, skinned, boned and minced or
   finely chopped
1 tbsp oil
1 small onion, finely chopped
½ green pepper, finely chopped
½-1 chilli, seeded and finely chopped
90g/3oz frozen sweetcorn
6 black olives, pitted and chopped
120ml/4fl oz double cream
Salt
12 prepared tortillas
Taco sauce (see recipe), guacamole and soured cream
   for toppings

1. Use a food processor or meat mincer to prepare the
chicken, or chop by hand.

2. Heat the oil in a medium frying pan and add the
chicken, onion and green pepper. Cook over moderate
heat, stirring frequently to break up the pieces of
chicken.

3. When the chicken is cooked and the vegetables are

Step 4 Place tortillas
slightly overlapping
on work surface and
fill with chicken.

Step 4 Use cocktail
sticks to secure
tortillas.

Step 5 Fry slowly
and turn carefully so
the filling does not
leak.

softened, add the chilli, sweetcorn, olives, cream and
salt. Bring to the boil over a high heat and boil rapidly,
stirring continuously, to reduce and thicken the cream.

4. Place 2 tortillas on a clean work surface, overlapping
them by about 5cm/2 inches. Spoon some of the
chicken mixture onto the tortillas, roll up and secure
with cocktail sticks.

5. Fry the flautas in about 1.25cm/½-inch oil in a large
frying pan. Do not allow the tortillas to get very brown.
Drain on kitchen paper.

6. Arrange the flautas on serving plates and top with
soured cream, guacamole and taco sauce.

Cook's Notes

Time
Preparation takes about 15
minutes and cooking takes about 15
minutes.

Variation
Green olives, may be substituted
for black, and red peppers for green.

Serving Idea
Flautas are often served with
rice, refried beans (see recipe) and a
salad.

AUBERGINE AND CHICKEN CHILLI

This unusual dish is both delicious and filling.

SERVES 4

2 medium aubergines
60ml/4 tbsps sesame oil
2 cloves garlic, crushed
4 spring onions
1 green chilli, finely chopped
340g/12oz boned and skinned chicken breast
60ml/4 tbsps light soy sauce
2 tbsps stock, or water
1 tbsp tomato purée
1 tsp cornflour
Sugar to taste

1. Cut the aubergines into quarters lengthways, using a sharp knife. Slice the aubergine quarters into pieces about 1.25cm/½-inch thick.

2. Put the aubergine slices into a bowl and sprinkle liberally with salt. Stir well to coat evenly. Cover with clingfilm and leave to stand for 30 minutes.

3. Rinse the aubergine slices very thoroughly under running water, then pat dry with a clean tea-towel.

4. Heat half of the oil in a wok, or large frying pan, and gently cook the garlic until it is soft, but not coloured.

5. Add the aubergine slices to the wok and cook, stirring frequently, for 3-4 minutes.

6. Using a sharp knife, slice the spring onions into thin diagonal strips. Stir the spring onions together with the chilli into the cooked aubergine, and cook for a further 1 minute. Remove the aubergine and onion from the pan, and set aside, keeping warm.

7. Cut the chicken breast into thin slices with a sharp knife.

8. Heat the remaining 2 tbsps of oil in the wok, and fry the chicken pieces for about 2 minutes or until they have turned white and are cooked thoroughly.

9. Return the aubergine and onions to the pan and cook, stirring continuously, for 2 minutes or until heated through completely.

10. Mix together the remaining ingredients and pour these over the chicken and aubergines in the wok, stirring constantly until the sauce has thickened and cleared. Serve immediately.

Step 6 Cut the spring onions diagonally into small pieces, about 1.25cm/½-inch long.

Cook's Notes

Time
Preparation takes about 10 minutes, plus 30 minutes standing time. Cooking takes about 15 minutes.

Cook's Tip
The vegetables can be prepared well in advance, but the aubergines should be removed from the salt after 30 minutes, or they will become too dehydrated.

Variation
Use turkey instead of chicken in this recipe, and courgettes in place of the aubergines.

CHICKEN MOGHLAI WITH CORIANDER CHUTNEY

The creamy spiciness of the chicken is a good contrast
to the hotness of the chutney.

SERVES 4-6

60ml/4 tbsps oil
1.4kg/3lbs chicken pieces, skinned
1 tsp ground cardamom
½ tsp ground cinnamon
1 bay leaf
4 cloves
2 onions, finely chopped
2.5cm/1-inch piece fresh root ginger, grated
4 cloves garlic, crushed
30g/1oz ground almonds
2 tsps cumin seeds
Pinch of cayenne pepper
280ml/½ pint single cream
90ml/6 tbsps natural yogurt
2 tbsps roasted cashew nuts
2 tbsps sultanas
Salt

Chutney
90g/3oz fresh coriander leaves
1 green chilli, chopped and seeded
1 tbsp lemon juice
Salt and pepper
Pinch of sugar
1 tbsp oil
½ tsp ground coriander

1. To prepare the chicken, heat the oil in a large frying pan. Fry the chicken pieces on each side until golden brown.

2. Remove the chicken and set aside. Put the

Step 7 Stir the yogurt, cashews and sultanas into the chicken. Heat through gently to plump up the sultanas, but do not allow the mixture to boil.

cardamom, cinnamon, bay leaf and cloves into the hot oil and meat juices and fry for 30 seconds. Stir in the onions and fry until soft but not brown.

3. Stir the ginger, garlic, almonds, cumin and cayenne pepper into the onions. Cook gently for 2-3 minutes, then stir in the cream.

4. Return the chicken pieces to the pan, along with any juices. Cover and simmer gently for 30-40 minutes, or until the chicken is cooked and tender.

5. Whilst the chicken is cooking, prepare the chutney. Put the coriander leaves, chilli, lemon, seasoning and sugar into a blender or food processor and work to a paste.

6. Heat the oil and cook the ground coriander for 1 minute. Add this mixture to the processed coriander leaves and blend in thoroughly.

7. Just before serving, stir the yogurt, cashews and sultanas into the chicken. Heat through just enough to plump up the sultanas, but do not allow the mixture to boil.

8. Serve at once with the coriander chutney.

Cook's Notes

Time
Preparation takes about 25 minutes, and cooking takes 30-40 minutes.

Watchpoint
Do not allow the curry to boil once the cream has been added.

Serving Ideas
Serve with boiled rice and a cucumber and tomato salad.

CHICKEN GUMBO

The African influence on Creole cuisine includes this soup-stew which takes its name from the African word for okra.

SERVES 4-6

120ml/4fl oz oil
1.4kg/3lb chicken, cut into 6-8 pieces
120g/4oz flour
2-3 dried red chillies or 1-2 fresh chillies, finely sliced
1 large onion, finely chopped
1 large green pepper, roughly chopped
3 sticks celery, finely chopped
2 cloves garlic, crushed
225g/8oz garlic sausage, diced
1 litre/1¾ pints chicken stock
1 bay leaf
Dash of Tabasco
Salt and pepper
120g/4oz fresh okra

Step 2 Continue cooking over low heat, stirring constantly as the flour begins to brown.

Step 3 When the flour is rich dark brown, add the remaining sauce ingredients.

1. Heat the oil in a large frying pan and brown the chicken on both sides, 3-4 pieces at a time. Transfer the chicken to a plate and set aside.

2. Lower the heat under the pan and add the flour. Cook over a very low heat for about 30 minutes, stirring constantly until the flour turns a rich, dark brown. Take the pan off the heat occasionally, so that the flour does not burn.

3. Add the chillies, onion, green pepper, celery, garlic and sausage to the pan and cook for about 5 minutes over a very low heat, stirring continuously.

4. Pour on the stock and stir well. Add the bay leaf, a dash of Tabasco and salt and pepper. Return the chicken to the pan, cover and cook for about 30 minutes or until the chicken is tender.

5. Top and tail the okra and cut each into 2-3 pieces. If the okra are small, leave them whole. Add to chicken and cook for a further 10-15 minutes. Remove the bay leaf and serve.

Cook's Notes

Time
Preparation takes about 30 minutes and cooking takes about 1 hour 25 minutes.

Cook's Tip
The oil and flour roux may be made ahead of time and kept in the refrigerator to use whenever needed. If the roux is cold, heat the liquid before adding.

Serving Idea
Serve on a bed of rice.

CORIANDER CHICKEN

Coriander Chicken is the perfect choice for any dinner party menu.

SERVES 4-6

1kg/2¼lbs chicken joints, skinned
2-4 cloves garlic, crushed
150g/5oz thick-set natural yogurt
75ml/5 tbsps cooking oil
1 large onion, finely sliced
2 tbsps ground coriander
½ tsp ground black pepper
1 tsp ground mixed spice
½ tsp ground turmeric
½ tsp cayenne pepper or chilli powder
120ml/4fl oz warm water
1 tsp salt
30g/1oz ground almonds
2 hard-boiled eggs, sliced
¼ tsp paprika

1. Cut each chicken joint into two, mix thoroughly with the crushed garlic and the yogurt. Cover the container and leave to marinate in a cool place for 2-4 hours or overnight in the refrigerator.

2. Heat the oil over a medium heat and fry the onion until golden brown. Remove with a slotted spoon and keep aside.

3. In the same oil, fry the coriander, ground pepper, ground mixed spice and turmeric for 15 seconds and add the chicken along with all the marinade in the container.

4. Fry the chicken for 5-6 minutes until it changes colour.

5. Add the cayenne or chilli powder, water, salt, and the fried onion slices. Bring to the boil, cover the pan and simmer for 30 minutes or until the chicken is tender.

6. Stir in the ground almonds and remove from heat. Garnish with the slices of egg and paprika.

Step 1 Cut each chicken joint into two, mix thoroughly with the crushed garlic and the yogurt.

Step 4 Adjust heat to medium-high and fry the chicken for 5-6 minutes until it changes colour.

Cook's Notes

Time
Preparation takes 20 minutes, plus 2-4 hours marinating. Cooking takes 45-50 minutes.

Watchpoint
Reduce the cooking time if boneless chicken is to be used.

CHICKEN TOMATO

Made with a very fragrant selection of spices,
this dish is sure to become a firm favourite.

SERVES 4-6

1 onion, chopped
3 tbsps oil
2.5cm/1-inch piece cinnamon stick
1 bay leaf
6 cloves
Seeds of 6 small cardamoms
2.5cm/1-inch piece fresh root ginger, grated
4 cloves garlic, crushed
1.4kg/3lb roasting chicken, cut into 8-10 pieces
1 tsp chilli powder
1 tsp ground cumin
1 tsp ground coriander
400g/14oz can tomatoes, chopped
1 tsp salt
2 sprigs fresh coriander leaves, chopped
2 green chillies, halved and seeded

Step 2 Fry the chicken and spices together, stirring continuously, to prevent the spices burning.

Step 3 Mix the canned tomatoes and remaining seasonings into the chicken, stirring thoroughly to blend the spices evenly.

1. In a large saucepan, fry the onion in the oil, until it has softened. Add the cinnamon, bay leaf, cloves, cardamom seeds, ginger and garlic. Fry for 1 minute.

2. Add the chicken pieces to the saucepan. Sprinkle the chilli powder, ground cumin and coriander over the chicken in the pan. Fry for a further 2 minutes, stirring continuously, to ensure the spices do not burn.

3. Stir in the remaining ingredients, mixing well to blend the spices evenly. Cover the pan and simmer for 40-45 minutes, or until the chicken is tender.

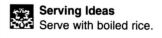

Cook's Notes

Time
Preparation takes about 30 minutes, and cooking takes about 40-50 minutes.

Preparation
If you ask your butcher, he will joint the chicken for you.

Serving Ideas
Serve with boiled rice.

MEXICAN KEBABS

Kebabs are a favourite barbecue food almost everywhere. The spice mixture and sauce gives these their Mexican flavour.

SERVES 4

460g/1lb pork or lamb, cut into 2.5cm/1-inch pieces
120g/4oz large button mushrooms, left whole
8 bay leaves
1 tsp cocoa powder
2 tsps chilli powder
1 tsp crushed garlic
½ tsp dried marjoram
Salt and pepper
90ml/6 tbsps oil
2 small onions, quartered
175g/6oz cooked rice
140ml/¼ pint Taco Sauce (see recipe)

Step 4 Place the kebabs on a lightly oiled rack on a grill pan and cook until the meat is tender and the onions are cooked. Baste frequently, using a small brush.

Step 1 Place the meat and mushrooms in a deep bowl with the marinade ingredients and stir to coat thoroughly.

1. Place the meat and mushrooms in a bowl. Add the bay leaves, cocoa, chilli powder, garlic, marjoram and seasoning to the oil and stir together. Pour over the meat and mix well. Coat all the beef and mushrooms.

2. Cover the bowl and leave to marinate at least 6 hours, preferably overnight.

3. Remove the meat, mushrooms and bay leaves from the marinade and reserve it. Thread the meat, mushrooms and bay leaves onto skewers, alternating the ingredients with the onions.

4. Place the kebabs on a lightly oiled grill pan and cook under a preheated grill for 15-20 minutes, turning frequently until cooked through. Baste often with the reserved marinade.

5. Mix the hot rice with the taco sauce and spoon onto a warm serving dish. Place the kebabs on top of the rice to serve.

Cook's Notes

Time
Preparation takes about 15 minutes, with at least 6 hours to marinate meat and mushrooms. Cooking time for the rice is about 8 minutes and 15-20 minutes for the meat.

Preparation
The kebabs may be cooked on a barbecue if wished.

Variation
Add pieces of red or green pepper, cherry tomatoes or sliced courgettes to the kebabs and cut meat into slightly smaller pieces so everything cooks in the same length of time.

SZECHUAN MEATBALLS

Szechuan is a region of China that lends its name to a style of cookery which includes many spices, most notably ginger. The spicy nature of these dishes means they require no salt.

SERVES 4

90g/3oz blanched almonds
460g/1lb minced beef
1 tsp grated fresh root ginger
1 clove garlic, crushed
½ large green pepper, finely chopped
Dash of Szechuan, chilli, or Tabasco sauce
2 tbsps soy sauce
Oil for frying
3 tbsps soy sauce
120ml/4fl oz vegetable stock
1 tbsp rice wine or white wine vinegar
2 tsps honey
1 tbsp sherry
1 tbsp cornflour
4 spring onions, diagonally sliced

1. Spread the almonds out evenly on a grill pan, and grill under a low heat for 3-4 minutes, or until lightly toasted. Stir the almonds often to prevent them from burning. Allow to cool, then chop coarsely using a large sharp knife.

2. In a large bowl, combine the chopped almonds with the meat, ginger, garlic, green pepper, Szechuan sauce,

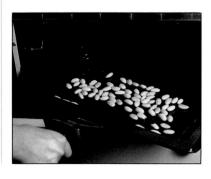

Step 1 Toast the almonds under a low grill until pale gold in colour, stirring them frequently to prevent them from burning.

Step 5 Gently fry the meatballs in the hot oil until they are evenly browned.

and the 2 tbsps of soy sauce. Use a wooden spoon, or your hands, to ensure that the ingredients are well blended.

3. Divide the mixture into 16 and roll each piece into small meatballs on a lightly floured board.

4. Heat a little oil in a large frying pan and lay in about half of the meatballs in a single layer.

5. Cook the meatballs over a low heat for about 20 minutes, turning them frequently until they are well browned all over.

6. Transfer to a serving dish and keep warm while you cook the remaining meatballs. Set aside as before.

7. Stir the 3 tbsps soy sauce, stock and vinegar into the frying pan and bring to the boil. Boil briskly for about 30 seconds. Add the honey and stir until dissolved.

8. Blend the sherry and cornflour together in a small bowl, and add this into the hot sauce. Cook, stirring constantly, until thickened.

9. Arrange the meatballs on a serving dish and sprinkle with the sliced spring onions. Pour the sauce over, and serve.

Cook's Notes

Time
Preparation takes about 20 minutes, cooking takes 40 minutes.

Serving Idea
Serve with boiled rice and a tomato salad.

Freezing
The meatballs will freeze uncooked for up to 3 months. The sauce should be prepared freshly when required.

SOUTHWESTERN STIR-FRY

East meets West in a dish that is lightning-fast to cook. Baby corn,
traditionally Oriental, echoes the American Southwestern love of corn.

SERVES 4

460g/1lb sirloin or rump steak
2 cloves garlic, crushed
90ml/6 tbsps wine vinegar
90ml/6 tbsps oil
Pinch of sugar, salt and pepper
1 bay leaf
1 tbsp ground cumin
Oil for frying
1 smal red pepper, sliced
1 small green pepper, sliced
60g/2oz baby corn
4 spring onions, shredded

Red Sauce
60ml/4 tbsps oil
1 medium onion, finely chopped
1-2 green chillies, finely chopped
1-2 cloves garlic, crushed
8 fresh ripe tomatoes, skinned, seeded and chopped
6 springs fresh coriander
3 tbsps tomato purée

Step 3 Cook the meat quickly over high heat to brown.

Step 3 Add the remaining ingredients and enough sauce to coat all ingredients thoroughly.

1. Slice the meat thinly across the grain. Combine in a plastic bag with the garlic, vinegar, oil, seasonings, bay leaf and cumin. Tie the bag and toss the ingredients inside to coat. Place in a bowl and leave about 4 hours.

2. Heat the oil for the sauce and cook the onion, chillies and garlic to soften but not brown. Add the tomatoes, coriander and tomato purée and cook about 15 minutes over gentle heat. Purée in a food processor until smooth.

3. Heat a frying pan and add the meat in three batches, discarding the marinade. Cook to brown and set aside. Add about 2 tbsps of oil and cook the peppers about 2 minutes. Add the corn and spring onions and return the meat to the pan. Cook a further 1 minute and add the sauce. Cook to heat through and serve immediately.

Cook's Notes

Time
Preparation takes about 25 minutes, with 4 hours for marinating the meat. The sauce takes about 15 minutes to cook and the remaining ingredients need about 6-7 minutes.

Preparation
The sauce may be prepared ahead of time and kept in the refrigerator for several days. It may also be frozen. Defrost the sauce at room temperature and then boil rapidly to reduce it again slightly.

Buying Guide
Fresh baby corn is available from greengrocers and supermarkets. It is also available canned in supermarkets and Oriental food stores.

FIVE-SPICE PORK (SEE KRONG MOO OB)

Serve this delicious, sweet, spicy Thai dish with plain rice.

SERVES 4

Red Curry Paste
12 small red chillies, chopped
3 cloves garlic, crushed
1 stem lemon grass
1 small onion, finely chopped
1 tsp grated fresh root ginger
2 tsps chopped fresh coriander stems and roots
Large pinch of cumin
1 tsp shrimp paste
2 tbsps oil

2 tbsps oil
1 tbsp Red Curry Paste
2 tbsps fish sauce
1 tbsp light soy sauce
2 tbsps sugar
1 tsp five-spice powder
1 tbsp chopped lemon grass
680g/1½lbs belly of pork slices, cut into 4cm/1½-inch chunks
Fresh coriander and lime twists to garnish

1. To make the red curry paste, place the chillies, garlic, lemon grass and onion in a pestle and mortar. Pound until the mixture is well bruised and the juices begin to blend.

2. Add all the remaining paste ingredients, except the oil, and continue to pound until a paste is formed.

Step 3 Stir the fish sauce, soy sauce, sugar, five-spice and lemon grass into the curry paste in the wok. Cook for 3 minutes.

Step 4 Add the pork to the ingredients in the wok and cook tossing frequently, for 10 minutes.

Finally, blend in the oil.

3. Heat the oil in a wok and fry the 1 tbsp curry paste for 2 minutes, stir in the fish sauce, soy sauce, sugar, five-spice powder and lemon grass. Cook for a further 3 minutes.

4. Add the pork to the wok and cook, tossing frequently for 10 minutes or until the pork is cooked through. Serve garnished with fresh coriander and lime twists.

Cook's Notes

Time
Preparation takes 10 minutes and cooking takes about 15 minutes.

Cook's Tip
The rind can be taken off the pork if preferred.

Preparation
Store the unused curry paste in a small air-tight jar in the refrigerator. The paste will keep for up to 1 month.

ENCHILADAS

Although fillings and sauces vary, enchiladas are one
of the tastiest Mexican dishes.

SERVES 6

10 ripe tomatoes, skinned, seeded and chopped
1 small onion, chopped
1-2 green or red chillies, seeded and chopped
1 clove garlic, crushed
Salt
Pinch of sugar
1-2 tbsps tomato purée
30g/1oz butter or margarine
2 eggs
280ml/½ pint double cream
340g/12oz minced pork
1 small red pepper, chopped
45g/4 tbsps raisins
30g/4 tbsps pine nuts
Salt and pepper
12 prepared tortillas (see recipe for Flour Tortillas)
30g/4 tbsps grated cheese
Sliced spring onions to garnish

1. Place the tomatoes, onion, chillies, garlic, salt, sugar and tomato purée in a blender or food processor and purée until smooth.

2. Melt the butter or margarine in a large saucepan. Add the purée and simmer for 5 minutes.

3. Beat together the eggs and cream, mixing well. Add a spoonful of the hot tomato purée to the cream and eggs and mix quickly. Return mixture to the saucepan and heat slowly, stirring constantly, until the mixture thickens. Do not boil.

4. While preparing the sauce, cook the pork and pepper slowly in a large frying pan. Use a fork to break up the meat as it cooks. Turn up the heat when the pork is

Step 3 Mix the eggs and cream with some of the hot sauce and then return it to the pan, stirring constantly.

nearly cooked and fry briskly for a few minutes. Add the raisins, pine nuts and seasoning.

5. Combine about a quarter of the sauce with the meat and divide the mixture evenly among all the tortillas. Spoon on the filling to one side of the centre and roll up the tortilla around it, leaving the ends open and some of the filling showing.

6. Place the enchiladas seam side down in a baking dish and pour over the remaining sauce, leaving the ends uncovered. Sprinkle over the cheese and bake in an oven preheated to 180°C/350°F/Gas Mark 4 for 15-20 minutes, or until the sauce begins to bubble. Sprinkle with the sliced onions and serve immediately.

Step 5 Spoon meat filling to one side of the tortillas and roll them up, leaving ends open.

Cook's Notes

Time
Preparation takes about 60 minutes to make the tortillas and about 30 minutes more to finish the dish.

Watchpoint
When preparing the sauce, do not allow it to boil once the egg and cream mixture has been added or it will curdle.

Economy
Left-over meat or chicken can be minced in a food processor or finely chopped and used in place of the freshly cooked meat.

CHILLI BEEF STEW

Beef, red onions, red peppers, paprika, tomatoes and
red beans all go into this zesty stew.

SERVES 6-8

Oil
900g/2lbs beef chuck steak, cut into 2.5cm/1-inch
   pieces
1 large red onion, coarsely chopped
2 cloves garlic, crushed
2 red peppers, cut into 2.5cm/1-inch pieces
1-2 red chillies, seeded and finely chopped
3 tbsps mild chilli powder
1 tbsp cumin
1 tbsp paprika
850ml/1½ pints beer, water or stock
225g/8oz canned tomatoes, puréed
2 tbsps tomato purée
225g/8oz canned red kidney beans, drained
Pinch of salt
6 ripe tomatoes, skinned, seeded and diced

1. Pour about 60ml/4 tbsps oil into a large saucepan or
flameproof casserole. When hot, brown the meat in
small batches over moderately high heat for about 5
minutes per batch.

2. Set aside the meat on a plate or in the lid of the
casserole. Lower the heat and cook the onion, garlic,
red peppers and chillies for about 5 minutes.

3. Add the chilli powder, cumin and paprika and cook
for 1 minute further. Pour on the liquid and add the
canned tomatoes, tomato purée and the meat.

4. Cover the casserole and cook slowly for about 1½-2
hours. Add the beans about 45 minutes before the end
of cooking time.

5. When the meat is completely tender, add salt to taste
and serve garnished with the diced tomatoes.

Step 2 Cook the
onions, garlic, red
peppers and chillies
slowly until slightly
softened.

Step 3 Add the liquid
to the pan. If using
beer, add it very
slowly as it will tend
to foam up in the
heat of the pan.

Cook's Notes

Time
Preparation takes about 25
minutes and cooking takes about 1½-2
hours.

Freezing
The chilli may be frozen for up to
3 months in a tightly covered freezer
container. Allow the chilli to cool
completely before sealing and
freezing. Defrost in the refrigerator and
bring slowly to the boil before serving.

Variation
The chilli may be made with pork
shoulder, or with a mixture of beef
and pork or minced beef or pork.

MEAT MADRAS

This hot curry is named after Madras, the major city in southern India.

SERVES 4-6

90ml/6 tbsps cooking oil
2 medium onions, coarsely chopped
2.5cm/1-inch fresh root ginger, peeled and coarsely chopped
3-4 cloves garlic, coarsely chopped
4-6 dried red chillies
2 large cloves garlic, crushed
1-2 fresh green chillies, sliced lengthways
225g/8oz canned tomatoes
3 tsps ground cumin
1 tsp ground coriander
½-1 tsp chilli powder
1 tsp ground turmeric
1kg/2¼lbs leg or shoulder of lamb, fat removed and meat cut into 4cm/1½-inch cubes
175ml/6fl oz warm water
1¼ tsps salt
1 tsp garam masala

1. Heat 3 tbsps of the oil over a medium heat and fry the onions, ginger, garlic and red chillies until the onions are soft, stirring frequently. Remove from heat and allow to cool.

2. Meanwhile, heat the remaining oil over medium heat and fry the crushed garlic and green chillies until the garlic is lightly browned.

3. Add half the tomatoes, along with the juice. Stir and cook for 1-2 minutes.

4. Add the cumin, coriander, chilli powder and turmeric, and cook for 6-8 minutes over a low heat, stirring frequently.

5. Add the meat, raise the heat and fry for 5-6 minutes, stirring, until meat changes colour.

6. Add the water, bring to the boil, cover and simmer for 30 minutes.

7. Place the fried onion mixture in a liquidiser or food processor and add the remaining tomatoes. Blend until smooth and add this to the meat. Bring to the boil, add the salt and mix well. Cover the pan and simmer for a further 35-40 minutes or until the meat is tender.

8. Stir in the garam masala and remove from heat.

Step 7 Blend the onion mixture and add to the meat.

Cook's Notes

Time
Preparation takes 25-30 minutes and cooking takes 1 hour 20 minutes.

Watchpoint
Meat Madras is meant to be hot, but if you prefer a milder flavour omit the chilli powder and remove the seeds from the chillies.

LEG OF LAMB WITH CHILLI SAUCE

Give roast lamb a completely different flavour with a spicy orange sauce.

SERVES 4

1kg/2¼lb leg of lamb
1 tbsp cornflour
Pinch of salt
Orange slices and coriander to garnish

Marinade
1 tsp cocoa powder
¼ tsp cayenne pepper
½ tsp ground cumin
½ tsp paprika
½ tsp ground oregano
140ml/¼ pint water
140ml/¼ pint orange juice
140ml/¼ pint red wine
1 clove garlic, crushed
2 tbsps brown sugar

1. If the lamb has a lot of surface fat, trim slightly with a sharp knife. If possible, remove the paper-thin skin on the outside of the lamb. Place the lamb in a shallow dish.

2. Mix together all the marinade ingredients and pour over the lamb, turning it well to coat completely. Cover and refrigerate for 12-24 hours, turning occasionally.

3. Drain the lamb, reserving the marinade, and place in a roasting tin. Cook in an oven preheated to 180°C/350°F/Gas Mark 4 for about 1½ hours or until meat is cooked according to taste. Baste occasionally with the marinade and pan juices.

4. Remove lamb to a serving dish and keep warm. Skim the fat from the top of the roasting tin with a large spoon and discard.

5. Pour the remaining marinade into the roasting tin and bring to the boil, stirring to loosen the browned meat juices. Mix the cornflour with a small amount of water and add some of the liquid from the roasting tin. Gradually stir cornflour mixture into the pan and bring back to the boil.

6. Cook, stirring constantly, until thickened and clear. Add more orange juice, wine or water as necessary.

7. Garnish the lamb with orange slices and sprigs of coriander. Pour over some of the sauce and serve the rest separately.

Step 6 Cook the sauce, stirring constantly, until thickened and clear. Add more orange juice, wine or water as necessary.

Cook's Notes

Time
Preparation takes about 15 minutes, plus 12-24 hours for the lamb to marinade. Cooking takes about 1½ hours for the lamb and 10 minutes to finish the sauce.

Cook's Tip
The marinade ingredients can also be used with beef or poultry.

Serving Ideas
Serve with rice or boiled potatoes and vegetables.

MUSSAMAN CURRY

This curry illustrates the Indian influence on some of Thailand's cuisine.

SERVES 4

4 cardamom pods
½ tsp coriander seeds
½ tsp caraway seeds
2 whole cloves
5 small red chillies, chopped
1 clove garlic, crushed
1 stem lemon grass, roughly chopped
2 spring onions, chopped
¼ tsp grated fresh root ginger
¼ tsp ground nutmeg
1 tbsp oil
Oil for shallow-frying
340g/12oz potatoes, peeled and cut into chunks
2-3 onions, peeled and cut into wedges
675g/1½lbs sirloin steak, cut into bite-size chunks
420ml/¾ pint coconut milk
2 tbsps dark muscovado sugar
1 tsp tamarind juice
Chopped coriander to garnish

Step 1 Crush the cardamom pods with the side of a knife and remove the seeds.

Step 2 Dry-fry the spices in a wok for 1 minute.

1. Crush the cardamom pods with the side of a knife and remove the seeds.

2. Place the coriander seeds, caraway seeds, cardamom and cloves in a wok and dry-fry for 1 minute, tossing frequently to prevent burning. Remove from the heat.

3. Mix the fried seeds, chillies, garlic, lemon grass, spring onions, ginger, nutmeg and oil together and pound in a pestle and mortar.

4. Heat the oil for shallow frying in a wok and fry the potato and onion wedges for 5 minutes or until they

begin to soften, then remove and set aside.

5. Add the meat to the pan and fry until browned. Stir in a quarter of the coconut milk and simmer gently for 30 minutes or until the meat is very tender.

6. Remove the meat from the wok with a slotted spoon and set aside. Add the chilli mixture to the wok and boil rapidly for 5 minutes, then blend in the remaining milk.

7. Return the meat, onions and potatoes to the wok. Stir in the sugar and tamarind juice and cook gently for 20 minutes. Garnish with chopped coriander.

Cook's Notes

Time
Preparation takes 25 minutes and cooking takes 1 hour.

Variation
Use lamb instead of beef in this recipe.

BEEF WITH TOMATO & PEPPER IN BLACK BEAN SAUCE

Black beans are a speciality of Cantonese cooking and give a pungent, salty taste to stir-fried dishes.

SERVES 6

2 large tomatoes
2 tbsps salted black beans
2 tbsps water
60ml/4 tbsps dark soy sauce
1 tbsp cornflour
1 tbsp dry sherry
1 tsp sugar
460g/1lb rump steak, cut into thin strips
1 small green pepper
60ml/4 tbsps oil
175ml/6fl oz beef stock
Pinch of black pepper

Step 4 Add the beef mixture to the hot wok and stir-fry until liquid ingredients glaze the meat.

1. Core tomatoes and cut them into 16 wedges. Crush the black beans, add the water and set aside.

2. Combine soy sauce, cornflour, sherry, sugar and meat in a bowl and set aside.

3. Cut the pepper into 1.25cm/½-inch diagonal pieces. Heat a wok and add the oil. When hot, stir-fry the green pepper pieces for about 1 minute and remove.

4. Add the meat and the soy sauce mixture to the wok and stir-fry for about 2 minutes. Add the soaked black beans and the stock. Bring to the boil and allow to thicken slightly. Return the peppers to the wok and add the tomatoes and pepper. Heat through for 1 minute and serve immediately.

Step 1 Remove cores from the tomatoes with a sharp knife. Cut into even-sized wedges.

Cook's Notes

Time
Preparation takes about 25 minutes, cooking takes about 5 minutes.

Watchpoint
Do not add the tomatoes too early or stir the mixture too vigorously once they are added or they will fall apart easily.

Variation
Substitute mange tout for the green peppers in the recipe. Mushrooms may also be added and cooked with the peppers or mange tout.

CHILLI CON CARNE

Although this dish is Mexican in origin, the version everyone knows best is really more American.

SERVES 4

1 tbsp oil
460g/1lb minced beef
2 tsps ground cumin
2 tsps mild or hot chilli powder
Pinch of oregano
Salt, pepper and pinch of sugar
1 tsp crushed garlic
2 tbsps flour
460g/1lb canned tomatoes
460g/1lb canned red kidney beans

1. Heat the oil in a large saucepan and brown the meat, breaking it up with a fork as it cooks.

2. Sprinkle on the cumin, chilli powder, oregano, salt, pepper and sugar, garlic and flour. Cook, stirring frequently, over a medium heat for about 3 minutes.

3. Add the tomatoes and their liquid and simmer 25-30 minutes.

4. Drain the kidney beans and add just before serving. Heat through for about 5 minutes.

Step 2 Sprinkle on the spice mixture and stir it into the meat. Skim off any fat that forms on the surface.

Step 3 Add the tomatoes and their liquid. Use a large spoon or potato masher to break up the tomatoes.

Cook's Notes

Time
Preparation takes about 15 minutes. Cooking takes about 40 minutes.

Serving Ideas
Spoon the chilli on top of boiled rice to serve or accompany with warm Flour Tortillas (see recipe). Top with a combination of soured cream, chopped onion, grated cheese or diced avocado.

Freezing
Allow the chilli to cool completely and place in rigid containers, seal, label and freeze for up to 3 months. Defrost thoroughly before reheating.

PORK WITH LIME AND CHILLI

Creamy coconut and fragrant spices blend together to
complement the pork beautifully.

SERVES 4

1 clove garlic, crushed
1 tsp brown sugar
1 tsp oil
1 tsp lime juice
1 tsp cornflour
460g/1lb lean pork, cut into 2.5cm/1-inch cubes
140ml/¼ pint oil for deep-frying
1 green chilli, seeded and thinly sliced
1 red chilli, seeded and thinly sliced
8 spring onions, trimmed and diagonally sliced
1 tsp ground turmeric
1 tsp ground coriander
1 tsp ground cumin
1 tsp ground nutmeg
Pinch of ground cloves
60ml/4 tbsps soy sauce
Grated rind and juice of 1 lime
140ml/¼ pint coconut cream
Salt and pepper

1. Combine the garlic, sugar, oil, lime juice and
cornflour in a large bowl. Stir in the cubed pork and coat
thoroughly with the garlic and lime juice mixture. Allow
to stand in the refrigerator for at least 1 hour.

2. Heat the oil for frying in a wok and add the pork
cubes. Cook, stirring frequently, for about 10 minutes
until golden brown and cooked through. Drain and set
aside.

3. Remove all but 1 tbsp of the oil from the wok. Reheat
and add the chillies and spring onions. Stir-fry for about
2 minutes.

4. Add the ground spices and fry for a further 30
seconds. Stir in the soy sauce, lime rind and juice,
coconut cream and seasoning and bring to the boil.

5. Add the fried pork to the sauce and heat through.
Adjust the seasoning and serve.

Step 1 Marinate the
pork in the garlic and
lime juice mixture for
at least 1 hour.

Step 3 Stir-fry the
spring onions and
chillies in about 1
tbsp of the oil for
about 2 minutes.

Cook's Notes

Time
Preparation takes about 20
minutes, plus at least 1 hour
marinating. Cooking takes about 20
minutes.

Cook's Tip
If you can't find canned coconut
cream in your local supermarket use
creamed coconut and follow the
directions on the packet.

Variation
Use chicken instead of the pork.

Serving Ideas
Serve on a bed of rice,
garnished with slices of lime.

ALBONDIGAS
(MEXICAN MEATBALLS)

A simple-to-make taco sauce makes plain meatballs a lot less ordinary
and a lot more fun to eat.

SERVES 4

225g/8oz minced veal
225g/8oz minced beef
1 clove garlic, crushed
2 tbsps dry breadcrumbs
½ chilli, seeded and finely chopped
½ tsp ground cumin
Salt and pepper
1 egg, beaten
Oil for frying
280ml/½ pint Taco Sauce (see recipe)
2 spring onions, chopped

1. Mix together the veal, beef, garlic, breadcrumbs, chilli, cumin and salt and pepper until well blended. Add the egg gradually to bind it together.

Step 2 Flour hands well and roll each piece into a ball.

Step 4 Brown the meatballs on all sides in hot oil until a good colour.

2. Turn the mixture out onto a floured surface and divide into 16 equal pieces. With floured hands, shape the mixture into balls.

3. Pour about 3 tbsps of oil into a large frying pan and place over high heat.

4. When the oil is hot, place in the meatballs and fry for 5-10 minutes until brown on all sides. Turn frequently during cooking.

5. Remove the browned meatballs and drain well on kitchen paper. Place in an ovenproof dish and pour in the taco sauce.

6. Heat through in an oven preheated to 180°C/350°F/ Gas Mark 4, for 10 minutes. Sprinkle with the chopped spring onions to serve.

Cook's Notes

Time
Preparation takes about 25 minutes and cooking about 20 minutes.

Serving Ideas
Serve with rice, Refried Beans (see recipe) or Guacamole (see recipe). Drizzle with soured cream if wished.

Freezing
Prepare and cook the meatballs and allow to cool completely. Place on baking sheets and freeze until firm. Transfer to freezer containers, label and store for up to 3 months. Defrost in the refrigerator and reheat thoroughly.

SPICED BEEF

Fragrant and spicy, this delicious Chinese dish is quick and easy to make.

SERVES 4

460g/1lb fillet of beef
1 tsp soft brown sugar
2-3 star anise, ground
½ tsp ground fennel
1 tbsp dark soy sauce
2.5cm/1-inch piece fresh root ginger, grated
½ tsp salt
2 tbsps vegetable oil
6 spring onions, sliced
1 tbsp light soy sauce
½ tsp freshly ground black pepper

Step 3 Put the sliced beef, ginger and salt into the marinade and stir well to coat evenly.

Step 1 Cut the beef into thin strips 2.5cm/1 inch long.

Step 5 Stir-fry the beef with the spring onions for 4 minutes.

1. Cut the beef, across the grain, into thin strips about 2.5cm/1-inch long.

2. In a bowl, mix together the sugar, spices and dark soy sauce.

3. Put the beef, ginger and salt into the soy sauce mixture and stir well to coat evenly. Cover and allow to stand for 20 minutes.

4. Heat the oil in a wok or large frying pan and stir-fry the spring onions quickly for 1 minute.

5. Add the beef and stir-fry for 4 minutes, or until the meat is well browned.

6. Stir in the light soy sauce and black pepper and cook gently for a further minute.

Cook's Notes

Time
Preparation takes about 15 minutes plus 20 minutes marinating. Cooking takes 5-6 minutes.

Variation
Add 120g/4oz sliced button mushrooms and 225g/8oz cooked Chinese egg noodles.

Preparation
Cutting the beef across the grain helps to keep it tender.

SPARERIBS IN CHILLI & CREAM SAUCE

Cocoa powder lends colour and depth to a sauce for ribs that's slightly more sophisticated than the usual barbecue sauce.

SERVES 4

1kg/2¼lbs pork spareribs
1 tsp cocoa powder
1 tbsp flour
½ tsp ground cumin
½ tsp paprika
½ tsp dried oregano, crushed
½-1 tsp chilli powder
Salt and pepper
280ml/½ pint warm water
2 tbsps thin honey
2 tbsps double cream
Lime wedges to garnish

1. Leave the ribs in whole slabs and roast in an oven preheated to 200°C/400°F/Gas Mark 6, for 20-25 minutes or until well browned. Drain off all the excess fat.

2. Blend together the cocoa, flour, cumin, paprika, oregano, chilli powder, seasoning, water and honey and pour over the ribs. Lower the temperature to 180°C/350°F/Gas Mark 4 and cook ribs for a further 30 minutes, until the sauce has reduced and the ribs are tender.

3. Place the ribs on a chopping board and using a large sharp knife, cut the ribs into pieces and arrange on a serving dish.

4. Pour the cream into the sauce in the roasting tin and place over a moderate heat. Bring to the boil and pour over the ribs. Garnish with lime wedges and serve.

Step 1 Cook the ribs until well browned. Remove from the roasting tin and pour off the fat.

Step 2 Cook the ribs until the meat is tender to the point of a knife and the sauce is reduced.

Step 3 Place ribs on a chopping board and cut into pieces.

Cook's Notes

Time
Preparation takes about 20 minutes, cooking takes 50-55 minutes.

Preparation
Ribs may be cooked for the last 30 minutes on an outdoor barbecue.

Serving Ideas
Serve with rice and an avocado or tomato salad.

SHAHI KORMA

The word 'Shahi' means royal, so this dish was probably created in the royal kitchens of the great Maharajas of India. The dish is rich and creamy and is a perfect choice for a special occasion.

SERVES 4-6

1kg/2¼lbs boned leg of lamb, trimmed and cut into
   4cm/1½-inch cubes
150g/5oz thick-set natural yogurt
1.25cm/½-inch piece fresh root ginger, peeled
   and grated
3-4 cloves of garlic, crushed
60g/2oz ghee or unsalted butter
2 medium onions, finely chopped

Spice Mixture
2 tbsps coriander seeds
8 whole green cardamom pods
10 whole black peppercorns
3-4 dried red chillies
1 tsp ground cinnamon
1 tsp ground mace

3 tbsps chopped fresh mint
60g/2oz ground almonds
280ml/½ pint warm water
½ tsp saffron strands, crushed
60g/2oz raw split cashews
140ml/¼ pint single cream
1 tbsp rose-water

1. Put the meat, yogurt, ginger and garlic into a large bowl. Mix thoroughly, cover and leave to marinate for about 2-4 hours.

2. Put the marinated meat, along with any marinade in a large heavy-based saucepan. Bring to a slow simmer, cover and cook for about 45-50 minutes, stirring occasionally. Transfer the meat to another container and keep it hot.

3. Grind the spice mixture together. Melt the ghee and fry the onions for a few minutes. Lower the heat and add the ground ingredients and the mint, stir and fry for 2-3 minutes.

4. Add half of the liquid in which the meat was cooked, stir and cook for 1-2 minutes. Add the ground almonds and the remaining meat stock, stir and cook for 1-2 minutes.

5. Add the meat, stir and fry over a medium heat for 5-6 minutes.

6. Add the water, saffron, 1½ tsps salt and the cashews. Bring to a slow boil, cover and simmer for 20 minutes.

7. Add the cream, stir and mix well, simmer uncovered for 6-8 minutes. Stir in the rose-water and remove from the heat.

Cook's Notes

Time
Preparation takes 20-25 minutes, plus 2-4 hours marinating. Cooking takes 1½ hours.

Watchpoint
Do not boil the korma after the cream has been added.

Preparation
Grind the spices in a spice mill or mini food processor or pound in a pestle and mortar.

CHILLI VERDE

A chilli, really a spicy meat stew, is as traditional in the Southwest of
America as it is in Mexico.

SERVES 6-8

Oil
900g/2lbs lean pork, cut into 2.5cm/1-inch pieces
3 green peppers cut into 2.5cm/1-inch pieces
1-2 green chillies, seeded and finely chopped
1 small bunch spring onions, chopped
2 cloves garlic, crushed
2 tsps chopped fresh oregano
3 tbsps chopped fresh coriander
1 bay leaf
850ml/1½ pints beer, water or chicken stock
225g/8oz canned chickpeas, drained
1½ tbsps cornflour mixed with 3 tbsps cold water
   (optional)
Salt and pepper
1 large ripe avocado
1 tbsp lime juice

1. Heat 60ml/4 tbsps of oil in a large flameproof
casserole and lightly brown the pork cubes in 2 or 3
batches over a high heat.

2. Lower the heat and cook the peppers to soften
slightly. Add the chillies, spring onions and garlic and
cook for 2 minutes.

3. Add the herbs and liquid and reduce the heat.
Simmer, covered, for 1-1½ hours or until the meat is
tender. Add the chickpeas during the last 45 minutes.

Step 1 The pork
should barely begin
to take on colour. Do
not over brown.

Step 4 If necessary,
add the cornflour
mixture to thicken the
chilli, stirring
constantly.

4. If necessary thicken with cornflour, stirring constantly
after adding until the liquid thickens and clears. Add salt
and pepper to taste and remove the bay leaf.

5. Peel and slice the avocado then quickly toss in
the lime juice and sprinkle over the top of the chilli to
serve.

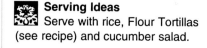

Cook's Notes

Time
Preparation takes about 30-40
minutes and cooking takes about 1-1½
hours.

Variation
Chicken or lamb make good
alternatives to pork.

Serving Ideas
Serve with rice, Flour Tortillas
(see recipe) and cucumber salad.

SHREDDED BEEF WITH VEGETABLES

Stir-fried food is recognised as being extremely nutritious and wholesome. This classic Chinese stir-fry is no exception, and has the bonus of being extremely quick and easy to prepare and cook.

SERVES 4

225g/8oz lean beef steak, cut into thin strips
½ tsp salt
60ml/4 tbsps vegetable oil
1 red and 1 green chilli, halved, seeded and sliced
1 tsp vinegar
1 stick celery, cut into thin 5cm/2-inch strips
2 carrots, cut into thin 5cm/2-inch strips
1 leek, white part only, sliced into thin 5cm/2-inch strips
2 cloves garlic, finely chopped
1 tsp light soy sauce
1 tsp dark soy sauce
2 tsps Chinese rice wine, or dry sherry
1 tsp caster sugar
½ tsp freshly ground black pepper

1. Put the strips of beef into a large bowl and sprinkle with the salt. Rub the salt into the meat and allow to stand for 5 minutes.

2. Heat 1 tbsp of the oil in a large wok. When the oil begins to smoke, reduce the heat and stir in the beef and the chillies. Stir-fry for 4-5 minutes.

3. Add the remaining oil and continue stir-frying the beef, until it turns crispy.

4. Add the vinegar and stir until it evaporates, then add the celery, carrots, leek and garlic. Stir-fry for 2 minutes.

5. Mix together the soy sauces, wine or sherry, sugar and pepper. Pour this mixture over the beef and cook for 2 minutes. Serve immediately.

Step 1 Put the finely sliced beef into a large bowl and sprinkle with salt. Rub the salt well into the meat and leave to stand.

Step 3 Add the remaining oil to the wok, and continue stir-frying the beef until it is crisp.

Step 5 Pour the soy sauce mixture over the beef and stir-fry rapidly for about 2 minutes, making sure that the beef and vegetables are well coated with the seasoning mixture.

Cook's Notes

Time
Preparation takes about 15 minutes, and cooking takes about 10 minutes.

Serving Ideas
Serve with plain boiled rice and prawn crackers.

Variation
Use your favourite combination of vegetables in place of those suggested in the recipe.

Watchpoint
Great care should be taken when preparing fresh chillies. Try not to get juice into the eyes or mouth. If this should happen, rinse well and with lots of cold water.

MINUTE STEAKS WITH TACO SAUCE

A quick meal needn't be ordinary. Prepare the taco sauce ahead and keep it on hand to add last-minute spice to a meal.

SERVES 6

280ml/½ pint Taco Sauce (see recipe)
30g/1oz butter or margarine
2 tbsps oil
6 minute steaks
Salt and pepper
120g/4oz button mushrooms, left whole
Chopped parsley or coriander leaves

Step 2 Add the mushrooms to the pan and cook briskly until lightly browned.

Step 1 Cook the steaks over a high heat until cooked to taste. To test, make a small cut in the centre of one steak.

1. Prepare the taco sauce according to the recipe directions. Heat the butter and oil together in a large frying pan, season the steaks with salt and pepper and fry 2 or 3 at a time for 2-3 minutes on each side, or until cooked to taste.

2. Remove the steaks to a warm serving dish and add the mushrooms to the pan. Sauté over a high heat to lightly brown them, then remove from the pan and keep warm.

3. Drain most of the fat from the pan and pour in the taco sauce. Place over a low heat until just bubbling. Spoon over the steaks.

4. Top the steaks with the sautéed mushrooms and sprinkle over parsley or coriander before serving.

Cook's Notes

Time
Preparation takes about 15 minutes. Cooking time takes 6-9 minutes per batch of steaks and about 10 minutes more to finish off the dish.

Variation
Substitute turkey escalopes for the steaks, if wished and cook until the juices run clear.

Serving ideas
Serve with rice or Flour Tortillas (see recipe).

Chapter 3
Side Dishes

FRIED BROWN RICE

This traditional Indian rice dish complements creamy curries perfectly.
White rice is actually used in this dish, the 'brown' in the title comes from
caramelised sugar!

SERVES 4-6

275g/10oz basmati rice
60ml/4 tbsps cooking oil
4 tsps sugar
1 tsp cumin seeds
2 cinnamon sticks broken up
6 whole cloves
6 black peppercorns
2 bay leaves, crumpled
570ml/1 pint water
1 tsp salt

1. Wash the rice and soak in cold water for 30 minutes. Drain well.

2. In a heavy-based saucepan, heat the oil over a medium heat and add the sugar.

3. The sugar will gradually begin to change colour to a caramel brown. As soon as it does, add the cumin seeds, cinnamon, cloves, black peppercorns and bay leaves. Fry for 30 seconds.

4. Add the drained rice and fry for about 5 minutes, stirring frequently and lowering the heat for the last minute or two.

5. Add the water and salt. Bring to the boil, cover and

Step 1 Wash the rice and soak in cold water for 30 minutes.

Step 3 As the sugar changes colour to caramel brown add the cumin seeds, cinnamon, cloves, black peppercorns and bay leaves.

simmer without lifting the lid for 12-15 minutes.

6. Remove the pan from heat and keep it undisturbed for a further 10-15 minutes before serving. Remove the cinnamon and bay leaves before serving.

Cook's Notes

Time
Preparation takes 5 minutes plus 30 minutes soaking time. Cooking takes 20-25 minutes.

Watchpoint
If the lid is lifted and the rice is stirred during cooking, the loss of steam will cause the rice to stick and turn soggy. Do not stir the rice immediately after it has been cooked, leave to stand to ensure dry and separate grains.

SHRIMP PASTE FRIED RICE
(KHAO CLOOK GAPI)

This is a strongly flavoured Thai rice dish which is best served with steamed vegetables.

SERVES 4

2 tbsps oil
30g/1oz dried shrimps
4 cloves garlic, crushed
2 red chillies, seeded and chopped
680g/1½lbs cooked rice
2 tbsps shrimp paste
2 eggs, beaten
4 spring onions, sliced
3 tbsps fish sauce
Coriander leaves, to garnish

1. Heat the oil in a wok and fry the dried shrimps for about 30 seconds, remove and set aside to drain on kitchen paper.

2. Add the garlic and chillies and fry until softened.

3. Stir in the rice and shrimp paste and stir-fry for 5 minutes or until heated through.

4. Add the beaten eggs and spring onions and cook over a low heat, stirring until the egg is cooked. Add the fish sauce.

5. To serve, sprinkle with the fried dried shrimps and garnish with coriander leaves.

Step 4 Add the beaten egg and spring onions to the rice. Cook over a low heat, stirring until the egg is cooked.

Step 1 Fry the dried shrimps for about 30 seconds.

Step 5 Sprinkle with the fried dried shrimps to serve.

Cook's Notes

Time
Preparation takes 10 minutes and cooking takes 15 minutes.

Serving Idea
Serve with vegetables such as steamed bok choy or long beans.

MATTAR PILAU

An easy to prepare pilau rice which has an attractive look provided by the rich green colour of the garden peas.

SERVES 4-6

275g/10oz basmati rice
90g/3oz ghee or unsalted butter
2 tsps fennel seeds
2-3 dried red chillies
6 whole cloves
2 cinnamon sticks, broken up
6 green cardamoms, split open the top of each pod
2 bay leaves, crumpled
1 large onion, finely sliced
175g/6oz frozen garden peas
1 tsp turmeric
1¼ tsps salt
570ml/1 pint water

1. Wash the rice and soak it in cold water for 30 minutes. Drain thoroughly.

2. Melt the ghee over a medium heat and fry the fennel seeds until they are light brown.

3. Add the chillies, cloves, cinnamon, cardamoms and bay leaves. Stir once and add the onion. Fry until the onion is lightly browned, stirring frequently.

4. Add the drained rice, peas, turmeric and salt. Stir and fry for 4-5 minutes until the rice is fairly dry, lowering the heat for the last 1-2 minutes.

Step 2 Melt the ghee over a medium heat and fry the fennel seeds until they are brown.

5. Add the water and bring to the boil. Cover the pan and simmer for 12-15 minutes. Remove the pan from heat and leave it undisturbed for a further 10-15 minutes. Remove the cinnamon, cardamom pods and bay leaves before serving.

Step 4 Add the rice, peas, turmeric and salt. Stir and fry until the rice is fairly dry.

Cook's Notes

Time
Preparation takes 10 minutes plus 30 minutes soaking time. Cooking takes 25-30 minutes.

Variation
Replace half the frozen peas with 90g/3oz frozen sweetcorn.

Watchpoint
Do not stir the rice or lift the lid while it is cooking.

FLOUR TORTILLAS

Tortillas made with wheat instead of corn are traditional in Northern Mexico.
Flour tortillas are easier to make and use than the corn variety.

MAKES 12

460g/1lb plain or wholemeal flour
1 tbsp salt
90g/3oz lard or white vegetable fat
280ml/½ pint hot water

1. Sift the flour and salt into a mixing bowl and rub in the lard until the mixture resembles fine breadcrumbs. Mix in the water gradually to form a soft, pliable dough. Wholemeal flour may need a little more water.

2. Knead on a well-floured surface until smooth and no longer sticky. Cover with a damp tea-towel.

3. Cut off about 45g/3 tbsps of dough at a time, keeping the rest covered. Knead into a ball.

4. Roll the ball of dough out into a very thin circle with a floured rolling pin. Cut into a neat round using a 25cm/10-inch plate as a guide. Continue until all the

Step 4 Roll out a ball of dough thinly and cut into a 25cm/10-inch circle.

dough is used.

5. Stack the tortillas as you make them, flouring each well to prevent sticking. Cover with a clean tea-towel.

6. Heat a heavy-based frying pan and carefully place in a tortilla. Cook for about 10 seconds per side. Stack and keep covered until all are cooked. Use according to chosen recipe.

Step 2 Knead a ball of prepared dough until smooth and pliable.

Step 6 Cook for 10 seconds per side in a hot frying pan.

Cook's Notes

Time
Preparation takes about 1 hour to make the dough and roll out all the tortillas, cooking takes about 5 minutes.

Serving Ideas
Use with any recipe that calls for tortillas. Also, serve hot as an accompaniment to any Mexican dish.

Freezing
Tortillas can be prepared and cooked in advance and frozen. Stack the tortillas between sheets of non-stick or wax paper. Place in plastic bags, seal, label and freeze for up to 2 months. Defrost at room temperature before using.

TANDOORI ROTI

Tandoori Rotis are traditionally cooked in the Tandoor – a barrel-shaped clay oven which distributes an even and fierce heat. They can be cooked in a hot conventional oven, and are equally delicious although the flavour is different.

MAKES 8

150g/5oz natural yogurt
460g/1lb plain flour
1 tsp sugar
1 tsp baking powder
½ tsp salt
1½ sachets fast-action yeast
1 tbsp ghee or 15g/½oz unsalted butter
1 medium egg, beaten
140ml/¼ pint warm milk

1. Beat the yogurt until smooth, and set aside.

2. In a large bowl, sift the flour with the sugar, baking powder, salt and yeast. Add ghee and mix thoroughly. Add the yogurt and egg and knead well.

3. Gradually add the warm milk and keep kneading until a smooth and springy dough is formed.

4. Place the dough in a large plastic food bag and tie up the uppermost part of the bag so that the dough has enough room to expand inside.

5. Rinse a large bowl with hot water and put the bag of dough in it. Place the bowl of in a warm place for ½-¾

hour when it will be almost double in volume.

6. Line a baking sheet with greaseproof paper or baking parchment.

7. Divide the dough into 8 equal-sized balls. Flatten each into cakes by pressing between your palms.

8. Dust each lightly in a little flour and roll out gently to 10cm/4-inch discs on the prepared baking sheet.

9. Bake on the top rung of an oven preheated to 225°C/450°F/Gas Mark 8 for 10-12 minutes. Cook in batches if necessary. Turn the rotis over and bake for a further 2 minutes.

Step 3 Gradually add the warm milk, and keep kneading until a smooth springy dough is formed.

Cook's Notes

Time
Preparation takes 10-15 minutes plus ½-¾ hour rising time. Cooking takes 10-15 minutes per batch.

Variation
Use wholemeal flour instead of plain flour. If necessary add a little extra milk if the dough seems dry.

Preparation
Use a steel, metal or enamel bowl for rising the dough as these will retain the heat better.

TACO SAUCE

This basic recipe has many uses in Mexican cooking – sauce, topping, dip or as an ingredient to give a dish extra flavour.

MAKES 280ML/½ PINT

1 tbsp oil
1 onion, diced
1 green pepper, diced
½-1 red or green chilli
½ tsp ground cumin
½ tsp ground coriander
½ clove garlic, crushed
Pinch of salt, pepper and sugar
400g/14oz can tomatoes
Tomato purée (optional)

1. Heat the oil in a heavy-based saucepan and when hot, add the onion and pepper. Cook slowly to soften slightly.

2. Finely chop the chilli, removing the seeds if wished. Add the chilli to the pan with the cumin, coriander and garlic and cook for 2-3 minutes.

Step 2 Cut the chilli in half, remove the seeds if wished, and chop the flesh finely.

3. Add the seasonings and sugar with the tomatoes and their juice. Break up the tomatoes with a fork or a potato masher.

4. Cook a further 5-6 minutes over a moderate heat to reduce and thicken slightly. Add tomato purée for colour, if necessary. Adjust seasoning and use hot or cold according to your recipe.

Step 3 Add remaining ingredients and use a potato masher or fork to break up tomatoes.

Step 4 Cook the sauce over a moderate heat to reduce and thicken.

Cook's Notes

Time
Preparation takes about 15-20 minutes, cooking takes about 8-10 minutes.

Serving Ideas
Use as a sauce or topping for fish, meat or poultry main dishes. Use in tacos, tostadas, nachos and as a dip for tortilla chips or vegetable crudités.

Freezing
Fill rigid containers with sauce at room temperature. Label and freeze for up to 3 months. Defrost at room temperature, breaking the sauce up as it thaws.

GUACAMOLE

This is one of Mexico's most famous dishes. It is delicious as a first course on its own or as an ingredient in other recipes.

SERVES 8

1 medium onion, finely chopped
1 clove garlic, crushed
Grated rind and juice of ½ lime
140ml/¼ pint Taco Sauce (see recipe)
3 large avocados
Pinch of salt
1 tbsp chopped fresh coriander
Coriander leaves to garnish
1 packet tortilla chips

1. Mix the onion, garlic, lime rind and juice and the taco sauce together in a large mixing bowl.

2. Cut the avocados in half lengthways. Twist the halves gently in opposite directions to separate.

3. Hit the stone with a large, sharp knife and twist the knife to remove the stone.

4. Place the avocado halves cut side down on a chopping board. Lightly score the skin lengthways and

Step 2 Cut avocados in half and twist the halves to separate.

Step 3 Hit the stone with a large knife and twist to remove the stone.

gently pull back to peel. Alternatively, scoop out avocado flesh with a spoon, scraping the skin well.

5. Chop the avocado roughly and immediately place in the bowl with the onion and lime.

6. Use a potato masher to break up the avocado until almost smooth. Do not over-mash. Season with salt and stir in the chopped coriander. Spoon into a serving bowl and garnish with coriander leaves.

7. Surround the bowl with tortilla chips for dipping.

Step 6 Use a potato masher to mash the avocado until nearly smooth.

Cook's Notes

Time
Preparation takes about 25 minutes.

Preparation
Do not prepare too long in advance. The avocado will darken even with the addition of lime juice if left too long.

Cook's Tip
Try leaving the avocado stone in the mixture. This is said to delay discolouration.

TARKA DHAL (SPICED LENTILS)

Dhal is a good source of protein and dhal of some sort is always cooked as part of a meal in an Indian household.

SERVES 4

175g/6oz Masoor dhal (red split lentils)
700ml/1¼ pints water
1 tsp ground turmeric
1 tsp ground cumin
1 tsp salt
30g/1oz ghee or unsalted butter
1 medium onion, finely chopped
2 cloves garlic, finely chopped
2 dried red chillies, coarsely chopped

1. Put the dhal, water, turmeric, cumin and salt into a saucepan and bring the liquid to the boil.

2. Reduce heat to medium and cook uncovered for 8-10 minutes, stirring frequently.

3. Now cover the pan and simmer for 30 minutes, stirring occasionally.

4. Remove the dhal from the heat, allow to cool slightly and mash through a sieve.

5. Melt the ghee or butter over medium heat and fry the onion, garlic and red chillies until the onion is well browned.

6. Stir in the half fried onion mixture to the dhal and put the dhal in a serving dish. Arrange the remaining fried onion on top.

Cook's Notes

Time
Preparation takes about 10 minutes and cooking takes about 50 minutes.

Serving Idea
Serve as an accompaniment to a curry with plain boiled rice.

SPICED CHICKPEAS

This very fragrant curry is delicious either on its own,
or as part of a larger Indian meal.

SERVES 6

460g/1lb chickpeas, soaked overnight in cold water
3 tbsps oil
1 large onion, chopped
2 bay leaves
2 green chillies, sliced in half lengthways
2.5cm/1-inch piece cinnamon stick
2.5cm/1-inch piece fresh root ginger, grated
4 cloves garlic, crushed
1½ tsps ground coriander
4 cloves, ground
1 tsp cumin seeds, ground
Seeds of 4 large black cardamoms, ground
Seeds of 4 green cardamoms, ground
280ml/½ pint canned chopped tomatoes
½ tsp salt
½ tsp black pepper
6 sprigs fresh coriander leaves, chopped

1. Cook the chickpeas in their soaking water, until they
are soft. Drain and reserve 225ml/8fl oz of the cooking
liquid.

2. Heat the oil in a frying pan and fry the onion gently,
until it is soft, but not coloured. Add the bay leaves,
chillies, cinnamon, ginger and garlic and fry for a further
1 minute.

3. Stir in the ground spices, the tomatoes and the salt
and pepper.

4. Add the reserved chickpea cooking liquid and the
drained chickpeas. Mix well. Sprinkle with the chopped
coriander leaves, cover and simmer for 10 minutes,
adding a little extra liquid, if necessary.

Step 1 Cook the chickpeas in their soaking water.

Step 2 Fry the bay leaves, cinnamon, ginger and garlic with the onion for 1 minute.

Step 4 Add the chickpeas to the sauce, cover and simmer for 10 minutes.

Cook's Notes

Time
Preparation takes about 15
minutes, plus overnight soaking.
Cooking takes about 45-50 minutes.

Preparation
Add 1 tsp of baking powder to
the chickpeas when soaking overnight,
to make them really tender. The
chickpeas can be cooked in a
pressure cooker for 10-15 minutes.

Watchpoint
Take great care not to get the
juice from the chillies into the eyes or
mouth. If this happens, rinse
thoroughly with cold water.

REFRIED BEANS

This is a classic accompaniment to both Mexican and Tex-Mex
main courses be they poultry or meat, vegetable or cheese.

SERVES 6-8

225g/8oz dried pinto beans
Water to cover
1 bay leaf
90ml/6 tbsps oil
Salt and pepper
120g/4oz grated mild cheese
Shredded lettuce
Flour Tortillas (see recipe)

1. Soak the beans overnight. Alternatively, bring the
beans to the boil in cold water and then allow to boil
rapidly for 10 minutes. Cover and leave to stand for 1
hour. Change the water, add the bay leaf and bring to
the boil. Cover and simmer about 2 hours, or until the
beans are completely tender. Drain the beans and
reserve a small amount of the cooking liquid. Discard
the bay leaf.

2. Heat the oil in a heavy-based frying pan. Add the
beans and, as they fry, start to mash them with the back
of a spoon. Do not overmash – about a third of the
beans should stay whole. Season to taste.

3. Smooth out the beans in the pan and cook until the
bottom is set but not browned. Turn the beans over and
cook the other side.

4. Top with the cheese and cook the beans until the
cheese melts. Serve with finely shredded lettuce and
tortillas, either warm or cut in triangles and deep-fried
until crisp.

Step 2 As the beans
fry in the oil, mash
them with the back of
a spoon.

Step 3 Turn the
beans over when the
bottom is set but not
brown.

Step 4 Sprinkle on
the cheese and cook
until it melts.

Cook's Notes

Time
Preparation takes about 15
minutes. The beans must be soaked
overnight or hydrated by the quick
method. The beans must be cooked at
least 2 hours before frying.

Watchpoint
Make sure the beans are
completely tender and have boiled
rapidly for at least 45 minutes before
eating.

Serving Ideas
Serve the beans as a side dish
with Enchiladas (see recipe) or with
barbecued meats.

AUBERGINES & PEPPERS SZECHUAN STYLE

Authentic Szechuan food is fiery hot. Outside China, restaurants often tone down the taste for Western palates.

SERVES 4

1 large aubergine
Oil for cooking
2 cloves garlic, crushed
2.5cm/1-inch piece fresh root ginger, shredded
1 onion, cut into 2.5cm/1-inch pieces
1 small green pepper, cut into 2.5cm/1-inch pieces
1 small red pepper, cut into 2.5cm/1-inch pieces
1 red or green chilli, seeded, and cut into thin strips
120ml/4fl oz chicken or vegetable stock
1 tsp sugar
1 tsp vinegar
Pinch of salt and Szechuan pepper
1 tsp cornflour
1 tbsp soy sauce
Dash of sesame oil

Step 2 Sprinkle lightly with salt and leave on kitchen paper or in a colander to drain.

colander or on kitchen paper for 30 minutes.

3. After 30 minutes, squeeze the aubergine gently to extract any bitter juices and rinse thoroughly under cold water. Pat dry and cut the aubergine into 2.5cm/1-inch cubes.

4. Heat about 3 tbsps oil in a wok. Add the aubergine and stir-fry for about 4-5 minutes. It may be necessary to add more oil as the aubergine cooks. Remove from the wok and set aside.

5. Reheat the wok and add 2 tbsps oil. Add the garlic and ginger and stir-fry for 1 minute. Add the onion and stir-fry for 2 minutes. Add the green pepper, red pepper and chilli and stir-fry for 1 minute. Return the aubergine to the wok.

6. Mix all the remaining ingredients together and add to the wok. Bring to the boil, stirring constantly, and cook until the sauce thickens and clears. Serve immediately.

Step 1 Cut aubergine in half and lightly score the surface.

1. Cut the aubergine in half and score the surface.

2. Sprinkle lightly with salt and leave to drain in a

Cook's Notes

Time
Preparation takes 15 minutes plus about 30 minutes standing time.

Cook's Tip
Salting the aubergine will help draw out any bitter juices.

Serving Suggestions
Serve as a vegetarian stir-fry dish with plain or fried rice, or serve as a side dish.

ALOO MATTAR

Aloo Mattar is a semi-moist potato dish which blends
easily with meat, chicken or fish curries.

SERVES 4-6

60ml/4 tbsps cooking oil
1 medium onion, finely chopped
2 cinnamon sticks, broken up
1.25cm/½-inch piece fresh root ginger, peeled and
    finely chopped
½ tsp ground turmeric
2 tsps ground cumin
¼ tsp chilli powder
¼ tsp freshly ground black pepper
460g/1lb potatoes, peeled and cut into 2.5cm/1-inch
    cubes
1-2 whole fresh green chillies
1 tbsp tomato purée
1 tsp salt
225ml/8fl oz warm water
120g/4oz frozen garden peas
1 tbsp chopped coriander leaves

1. Heat the oil in a frying pan over medium heat and fry onion, cinnamon and ginger for 4-5 minutes, stirring frequently.

2. Reduce heat to low and add the turmeric, cumin, chilli powder and black pepper. Stir and fry for 1 minute.

3. Add the potatoes and the green chillies, stir and cook for 2-3 minutes until the spices are blended thoroughly.

4. Stir in the tomato purée and salt.

5. Add the water, bring to the boil, cover the pan and cook over medium to low heat for 10 minutes until the potatoes are half cooked.

6. Add the peas, cover the pan and cook until the potatoes are tender.

7. Remove the pan from the heat, stir in half the chopped coriander leaves and sprinkle the remainder on top.

Cook's Notes

Time
Preparation takes 10-15 minutes and cooking takes 25-30 minutes.

Cook's Tip
Use a waxy variety of potatoes for the best results.

Variation
Use a mixture of potatoes and cauliflower florets.

SPICY ORIENTAL NOODLES

A most versatile vegetable dish, this can be served with meat or
on its own for a vegetarian main course.

SERVES 4

225g/8oz Chinese noodles (medium thickness)
75ml/5 tbsps oil
4 carrots, peeled
225g/8oz broccoli
12 dried Chinese mushrooms, soaked in warm water
   for 30 minutes
4 spring onions, diagonally sliced
1 clove garlic
1-2 tsps chilli sauce, mild or hot
60ml/4 tbsps soy sauce
60ml/4 tbsps rice wine or dry sherry
2 tsps cornflour

1. Cook the noodles in boiling salted water for about 4-5 minutes. Drain well, rinse under hot water to remove starch and drain again. Toss with about 1 tbsp of the oil to prevent sticking.

2. Using a large, sharp knife, slice the carrots thinly on the diagonal.

3. Cut the florets off the stems of the broccoli and divide into even-sized but not too small sections. Slice the stalks thinly on the diagonal. If they seem tough, peel them before slicing.

4. Place the carrots and broccoli in boiling water for about 2 minutes to blanch. Drain and rinse under cold water to stop the cooking, and leave to drain dry.

5. Remove and discard the mushroom stems and slice the caps thinly. Set aside with the spring onions.

6. Heat a wok and add the remaining oil with the garlic clove. Leave the garlic in the pan while the oil heats and then remove it. Add the carrots and broccoli and stir-fry about 1 minute. Add the mushrooms and spring onions and continue to stir-fry, tossing the vegetables in the pan continuously.

7. Combine the chilli sauce, soy sauce, wine and cornflour, mixing well. Pour over the vegetables and cook, stirring, until the sauce clears. Toss with the noodles to heat them through and serve immediately.

Step 7 Cook the vegetables and sauce ingredients until the cornflour thickens and clears.

Cook's Notes

Time
Preparation takes about 25 minutes and cooking takes about 7-8 minutes.

Serving Ideas
Use as a side dish with chicken, meat or fish, or serve as a starter. May also be served cold as a salad.

LONG BEANS IN COCONUT MILK

In this recipe long beans are lightly cooked so that they are still slightly crunchy when served.

SERVES 4-6

460g/1lb long beans
1 tbsp oil
2 stems lemon grass, sliced
2.5cm/1-inch piece galangal, sliced into thin sticks
1 large red chilli, seeded and chopped
280ml/½ pint thin coconut milk

Step 2 Stir-fry the lemon grass, galangal and chilli for 1 minute.

Step 1 Cut the beans into 5cm/2-inch pieces.

Step 3 Add the coconut milk to the wok. Bring to the boil and boil for 3 minutes.

1. Top and tail the beans and cut into 5cm/2-inch pieces.

2. Heat the oil in a wok and stir-fry the lemon grass, galangal and chilli for 1 minute.

3. Add the coconut milk and bring to the boil. Boil for 3 minutes.

4. Stir in the beans, reduce the heat and simmer for 6 minutes.

Cook's Notes

Time
Preparation takes 10 minutes and cooking takes 7 minutes.

Variation
Substitute mange tout peas for the beans and reduce the cooking time to 2-3 minutes.

Preparation
If long beans are unavailable, use French beans instead.

GOBI MATTAR
(CABBAGE WITH GARDEN PEAS)

This quick and easy side dish is the ideal accompaniment for Meat Madras.

SERVES 4-6

340g/12oz green cabbage
3 tbsps cooking oil
¼ tsp black mustard seeds
½ tsp cumin seeds
10-12 fenugreek seeds
2-4 dried red chillies, whole
1 small onion, finely sliced
½ tsp ground turmeric
120g/4oz frozen garden peas
¾ tsp salt
1 tsp ground coriander
¼-½ tsp chilli powder
2 small ripe tomatoes, skinned and chopped
1 tbsp chopped coriander leaves

1. Shred or chop the cabbage finely.

2. Heat the oil in a large frying pan over medium heat and fry the mustard seeds until they pop.

3. Add the cumin seeds followed by the fenugreek, red chillies and the onion. Stir and fry until the onion is soft.

4. Stir in the turmeric and add the cabbage. Stir and mix thoroughly.

5. Add the peas and salt, stir and cover the pan. Lower heat to minimum and cook for 5 minutes.

6. Add the ground coriander, the chilli powder and the chopped tomatoes. Stir until it is completely dry.

7. Remove from heat and stir in half the coriander leaves.

8. Put the cabbage into a serving dish and sprinkle the remaining coriander leaves on top.

Step 1 Shred or chop the cabbage finely.

Step 6 Add the ground coriander, the chilli powder and the chopped tomatoes.

Cook's Notes

Time
Preparation takes 15 minutes, cooking takes 10-15 minutes.

Cook's Tip
Use a non-stick frying pan.

Chapter 4
Desserts

Mango Fool • Spiced Fruit Salad • Kulfi

Coconut and Banana Pancakes • Almond Float with Fruit

Guava Mint Sorbet

MANGO FOOL

To cool the palate after a spicy meal, the taste of mango,
lime, ginger and cream is perfect.

SERVES 6

2 large ripe mangoes
1 small piece fresh root ginger, peeled and shredded
120g/4oz sifted icing sugar
Juice of ½ lime
280ml/½ pint double cream

1. Cut the mangoes in half, cutting around the large central stone. Reserve two slices. Scoop out the remaining flesh into a blender or food processor.

2. Add the ginger, icing sugar and lime juice and purée in the blender or food processor until smooth.

3. Whip the cream until soft peaks form and fold into the mango purée.

4. Divide the mixture between 6 glass serving dishes and leave in the refrigerator for 1 hour before serving.

5. Cut the reserved mango slices into 6 smaller slices or pieces and use to decorate the fools.

Step 3 Whisk the cream to soft peaks.

Step 1 Cut the mango in half, slicing around the stone. Scoop out pulp.

Step 3 Fold the cream into the mango purée using a large spoon or rubber spatula.

Cook's Notes

Time
Preparation takes about 20 minutes. The fool should be refrigerated 1 hour before serving.

Serving Ideas
Accompany with biscuits.

Watchpoint
When whipping cream, refrigerate it for at least 2 hours before use for best results.

SPICED FRUIT SALAD

Sweet and spicy, this fruit salad is certainly out of the ordinary.
SERVES 6

1 mango, peeled and cubed
1 small pineapple, skinned, cored and cubed
2 bananas, peeled and sliced
12 lychees, peeled and stones removed
2 kiwi fruit, peeled and sliced
1 small melon, peeled and cubed
2 oranges, peeled and segmented
120g/4oz palm sugar or light brown sugar
1 tsp tamarind extract
2 tbsps water
Juice of 1 lime
2.5cm/1-inch piece fresh ginger, grated
½ tsp ground nutmeg
¼ tsp ground cinnamon
¼ tsp ground coriander

1. Prepare all the fruit over a bowl, to catch the juice.

Step 1 Prepare the fruit over a bowl, so that the juice can be caught and used in the fruit salad.

Step 2 Combine the spices with the liquids, mixing them together well to blend thoroughly.

Step 2 Stir the spicy juice mixture thoroughly into the prepared fruit.

Arrange the prepared fruit in a serving bowl.

2. In a small bowl, combine the sugar with the tamarind, water, lime juice and spices. Stir this into the prepared fruit, together with any fruit juice, mixing well to blend thoroughly.

3. Chill the fruit salad for at least 1 hour before serving, stirring it again before you do.

Cook's Notes

Time
Preparation takes about 30 minutes, plus chilling time of at least 1 hour.

Cook's Tip
If tamarind extract is unobtainable, substitute the juice of ½ lemon and omit the water as well.

Variation
Use whatever types of exotic fruit are available or substitute more common types.

KULFI
(INDIAN ICE CREAM)

Kulfi is by far the most popular ice cream in India. It is firmer than conventional ice cream and is usually set in small tin or aluminium moulds. You can, however, use either small yogurt pots or a plastic ice cream tub.

SERVES 6-8

140ml/¼ pint milk
2 tbsps ground rice
1 tbsp ground almonds
450ml/14½oz can evaporated milk
1 tsp ground cardamom seeds
60g/2oz sugar
420ml/¾ pint double cream
1 tbsp rose-water
30g/1oz shelled, unsalted pistachio nuts, lightly crushed

1. Heat the milk until it is lukewarm.

2. Put the ground rice and ground almonds into a small bowl and gradually add the warm milk, a little at a time, and make a thin paste of pouring consistency. Stir continuously and break up any lumps, if any lumps remain, sieve the paste.

3. Heat the evaporated milk to boiling point and add the ground cardamom.

4. Take the pan off the heat and gradually add the almond/rice mixture, stirring continuously.

5. Add the sugar and cream and place the pan over medium heat, cook the mixture for 12-15 minutes, stirring continuously. Remove the pan from heat and allow the mixture to cool slightly.

6. Add the rose-water and half of the pistachio nuts, stir and mix well. Allow the mixture to cool completely, stirring frequently to prevent a skin from forming on the surface.

7. When the mixture has cooled completely, put it into a plastic ice cream box or individual moulds.

8. Top with the remaining pistachio nuts and place in the freezer for 4-5 hours or until frozen.

9. Place the kulfi in the refrigerator before serving. This will soften the kulfi slightly and will make it easier to cut into the required size when it is set in an ice cream tub. The time required to soften the kulfi will vary according to the size of the container used.

Cook's Notes

Time
Preparation takes 10 minutes, cooking takes 15-20 minutes. Freeze for at least 4-5 hours.

Variation
Instead of using rose-water add 5-6 drops of vanilla or almond essence.

COCONUT AND BANANA PANCAKES

These pancakes are delicious served warm or cold.

SERVES 4

120g/4oz rice flour
Pinch of salt
2 eggs
280ml/½ pint thin coconut milk
Green food colouring (optional)
30g/1oz shredded or desiccated coconut

Filling
Grated rind of ½ lime
2 tbsps lime juice
1 tsp sugar
1 tbsp shredded or desiccated coconut
2 bananas

Oil for frying

1. Place the flour and the salt in a mixing bowl and make a well in the centre. Drop in the eggs and a little of the coconut milk.

2. Using a wooden spoon beat well, slowly incorporating the flour until you have a smooth, thick paste.

3. Gradually beat in the remaining coconut milk. Stir in a few drops of food colouring. Allow to stand for 20 minutes.

4. Meanwhile, make the filling. Mix together the lime rind, juice, sugar and coconut. Slice the bananas and toss in the mixture.

Step 1 Place the flour and salt in a mixing bowl and make a well in the centre. Drop in the eggs and a little of the milk.

Step 5 Spoon about 60ml/4 tbsps of pancake batter into the pan and swirl to coat.

5. Stir the coconut into the pancake batter and heat a little oil in a 20.5cm/8-inch heavy-based frying pan. Pour off the excess and spoon in about 60ml/4 tbsps of the batter. Swirl to coat the pan. Cook for about 1 minute or until the underside is golden.

6. Flip or toss the pancake over and cook other side. Slide the pancake out of the pan and keep warm. Repeat until all the batter is used. Fill the pancakes with the banana mixture and serve immediately.

Cook's Notes

Time
Preparation takes 15 minutes, plus 20 minutes standing time.

Serving Ideas
Fold the pancakes into quarters and spoon some filling inside or divide filling between the pancakes and roll up.

ALMOND FLOAT WITH FRUIT

Sweet dishes are not often served in the course of a Chinese meal. Banquets are the exception, and this elegant fruit salad is certainly special enough.

SERVES 6-8

1 envelope gelatine
90ml/6 tbsps cold water
90g/3oz sugar
280ml/½ pint milk
1 tsp almond essence
Few drops of red or yellow food colouring (optional)

Almond Sugar Syrup
90g/3oz sugar
570ml/1 pint water
½ tsp almond essence
Fresh fruit such as kiwi, mango, pineapple, bananas, lychees, oranges or satsumas, peaches, berries, cherries, grapes or starfruit
Fresh mint to decorate

1. Allow the gelatine to soften in the cold water for about 10 minutes or until spongy. Put in a large mixing bowl.

2. Bring 175ml/6fl oz water to the boil and stir in the sugar. Cool slightly then pour into the gelatine and water mixture and stir until the gelatine and sugar dissolve.

3. Add the milk, almond essence and food colouring, if using. Mix well and pour into a 20cm/8-inch square baking tin. Chill in the refrigerator until set.

4. Mix the sugar and water for the syrup together in a heavy-based pan. Cook over gentle heat until the sugar dissolves. Bring to the boil and allow to boil for about 2 minutes, or until the syrup thickens slightly. Add the almond essence and allow to cool at room temperature. Chill in the refrigerator until ready to use.

5. Prepare the fruit and place in an attractive serving dish. Pour over the chilled sugar syrup and mix well.

6. Cut the set almond float into 2.5cm/1-inch diamond shapes. Use a spatula to remove them from the pan and stir them gently into the fruit mixture. Decorate with sprigs of fresh mint to serve.

Step 2 Add the hot water and sugar mixture to the soaked gelatine, and stir until the mixture is clear and not grainy.

Step 6 Cut the set almond float mixture into diamonds and remove from the tin with a palette knife.

Cook's Notes

Time
Preparation takes about 25 minutes. The almond float will need about 2 hours to set.

Preparation
To prepare kiwi fruit, peel and cut into thin rounds. Peel lychees, cut around the stone or leave in. Peel mangoes and cut into thin slices around the large stone. Cut starfruit crossways into thin slices.

Buying Guide
Use whatever fruits are in season at the moment, or use good quality canned fruit. Exotic fruits are available in most large supermarkets and some greengrocers. Allow about 900g/2lbs of fruit for 6-8 people.

GUAVA MINT SORBET

When a light, refreshing dessert is called for, a sorbet can't be surpassed.
The exotic taste of guava works well with mint.

MAKES 850ML/1½ PINTS

175g/6oz granulated sugar
280ml/½ pint water
4 ripe guavas
2 tbsps chopped fresh mint
Lime juice to taste
1 egg white
Fresh mint leaves to decorate

1. Combine the sugar and water in a heavy-based saucepan and bring slowly to the boil to dissolve the sugar. When the mixture is a clear syrup, boil rapidly for 30 seconds. Allow to cool to room temperature and then chill in the refrigerator.

2. Cut the guavas in half and scoop out the pulp. Discard the skins and seeds and purée the fruit until smooth in a liquidiser or food processor. Add the mint and combine with the cold syrup. Add lime juice until the right balance of sweetness is reached.

3. Pour the mixture into a shallow container and freeze until slushy. Process again to break up the ice crystals and then freeze until firm.

4. Whip the egg white until stiff but not dry. Process the sorbet again and when smooth, add the egg white. Fold in gently then freeze again until firm.

5. Remove from the freezer 15 minutes before serving and keep in the refrigerator. Scoop out and decorate each serving with mint leaves.

Step 2 Combine the puréed guava, mint and cold syrup.

Step 3 Freeze the mixture until slushy and then process to break up the ice crystals.

Step 4 Process the frozen mixture again and gradually fold in the egg white.

Cook's Notes

Time
Preparation takes about 2-3 hours, allowing the sorbet to freeze in between processing.

Freezing
The sorbet will keep in the freezer for up to 3 months in a well-sealed, rigid container.

Index